D1290006

The Pursuit of Laziness

The Pursuit of Laziness

An Idle Interpretation of the Enlightenment

Pierre Saint-Amand

Translated by Jennifer Curtiss Gage

PRINCETON UNIVERSITY PRESS

Princeton and Oxford

Published by Princeton University Press, 41 William Street, Princeton,
New Jersey 08540

In the United Kingdom: Princeton University Press, 6 Oxford Street,
Woodstock, Oxfordshire OX20 1TW

press.princeton.edu

Library of Congress Cataloging-in-Publication Data
Saint-Amand, Pierre, 1957–
The pursuit of laziness : an idle interpretation of the Enlightenment /
Pierre Saint-Amand ; translated by Jennifer Curtiss Gage.
p.   cm.
Includes bibliographical references and index.
ISBN 978-0-691-14927-1 (hardcover : alk. paper)   1. Enlightenment—France.
2. Laziness. I. Title. II. Title: Idle interpretation of the Enlightenment.
B802.S25 2011
190.9′033—dc22   2010036754

British Library Cataloging-in-Publication Data is available

This book has been composed in Garamond Premier Pro
Printed on acid-free paper. ∞
Printed in the United States of America

1 3 5 7 9 10 8 6 4 2

The Idler, though sluggish, is yet alive, and may sometimes be

stimulated to vigor and activity. He may descend into profound-

ness, or tower into sublimity; for the diligence of the Idler is

rapid and impetuous, as ponderous bodies forced into velocity

move with violence proportionate to their weight.

—Samuel Johnson, *The Idler*, Numb. 1, Saturday, April 15, 1758

Contents

CONTENTS

Acknowledgments

This book has been long in the making. My own laziness might be partly to blame. But I would like to thank those who supported the project and have been patient in seeing it through: Nancy Armstrong and Len Tennenhouse, Marcel Hénaff, Ourida Mostefai, Virginia Krause, Jacques Khalip, Dena Goodman, Susan Stewart, and Sina Najafi. I had the opportunity to present materials from this book at different venues. They include: the University of Pennsylvania, Cornell University, the French Culture Workshop at Stanford University, the University of Notre Dame, Johns Hopkins. I thank all those who guided me with suggestions along the way.

I could not be more grateful to Rob Tempio at Princeton University Press for his early interest, encouragement, and the care with which he followed through. This book could not especially be what it is without the comments and helpful suggestions from the two anonymous readers. They offered enlightening ways to better the manuscript and they have my infinite gratitude. All remaining shortcomings are of course my own entirely. As always, I owe a special debt of recognition to my translator, Jennifer Curtiss Gage, for her gift of words, her patience, meticulousness, and her fidelity. I am grateful to the Office of Vice President of Research at Brown University for providing the grants toward the translation. Finally, my thanks are due to Karen Verde for her methodical and careful editing as well as to David Luljak for preparing the index.

A part of the third chapter appeared previously as "Freedom and the Project of Idleness" in *Rousseau and Freedom*, ed. Christie McDonald and Stanley Hoffman (Cambridge: Cambridge University Press, 2010), 245–256. It is reprinted with permission of the Press. An early version of a section of the third chapter appeared as "*Reveries* of Idleness" in *Approaches to Teaching Rousseau's "Confessions" and "Reveries,"* ed. Ourida Mostefai and John O'Neil (New York: Modern Language Association of America, 2003), 127–131.

The Pursuit of Laziness

Introduction

Idle Nation

"Ours is the century of laziness," announces Louis-Sébastien Mercier in *Mon bonnet de nuit* (*My Nightcap*, 1784).[1] Looking back upon the literary production of the eighteenth century, he nostalgically observes the waning of the grand intellectual projects. The age of massive tomes of philosophy, of erudite abstraction, is past; the century has now discovered the trifle, the trivial. Mercier laments the impatience of authors and readers alike. It is as if the time of work has been compressed, interrupted by the futile. He would like to restore this time to the artist, so that creation could be reclaimed through action. Mercier concludes with a morality based on usefulness and fecundity, for a proper culture of "enlightenment."

This despondent view of the century, in particular of intellectual work, might divert us from the image of a century known for bringing about a massive systematization of work, a valorization of labor that culminated in the birth of industrial capitalism. Indeed, the eighteenth century was the century of industry; as such it trumpeted the cause of action and energy. Severe measures aimed at repressing idlers remained in place for the duration of the century, alongside new strategies for economic emancipation. Such repression sought justification through various discourses, beginning with the religious. One text that exerted an influence throughout the eighteenth century (as many as four editions were published in 1743) was Antoine de Courtin's *Traité de la paresse* (*Treatise on Laziness*), in which he condemns laziness in the harshest terms.[2] Christian in inspiration, Courtin's treatise considers laziness strictly as a defect: it is an obstacle to (good) works, it diverts one from a useful life, from action understood as a principle of creation. In the author's apt phrase, laziness is nothing less than "the devil's couch of ease."[3] More precisely, Courtin defines laziness as "a numbness, a despondency, a desolation, a weight that depletes courage and instills a repugnance for all good deeds; its hatred for work is equal to its love of rest" (*Traité*, p. 28). The moralist sets himself the task of correcting this deadly inclination by inspiring active virtues, those of work as a duty imposed by God. For Courtin the key, in his striking phrase, is not to allow others "the leisure to enjoy leisure" (*Traité*, Avertissement, p. 5). To set man on the right path, the moralist does not hesitate to invoke a mythological model: the paragon of virtue that he proposes is none other than Hercules, the action hero par excellence.

These same values circulate in the Enlightenment discourse of emancipation, as voiced by the encyclopedists. The Chevalier Louis de Jaucourt translated the religious condemnation of inactivity into secular terms.[4] Under the term "oisiveté" (idleness), Jaucourt lumps unemployment together with loafing. He understands the former literally as a lack of occupation, a void, a pure negativity. Jaucourt at once universalizes and naturalizes work as both a bodily need and a social duty: "the human spirit, being of an active nature, cannot remain in a state of inaction," he writes. Idleness, by contrast, is a "source of disorder"; it strikes at the heart of good citizenship, and may lead to criminal deeds. Like Courtin, Jaucourt celebrates Hercules as the timeless hero of work, the very model of work as pleasure.[5]

In his article on "Paresse" for the *Encyclopédie* of Diderot and d'Alembert, Jaucourt makes an effort to distinguish between "paresse" (laziness) and "fainéantise" (loafing), which, despite their close synonymy, denote for him two different degrees of wrongdoing. If laziness concerns (the lack of) action in mind and body alike, loafing is a vice of the body alone. For him the lazy man is matter reduced to inaction, and this physical inaction reverberates in the "character of the soul." The loafer or good-for-nothing, in contrast, "likes to be idle, he hates occupation, and avoids work."[6] The loafer's perversion is thus to convert the pleasure of work into its opposite. The negativity of *far niente* is literally *nothingness*. Like Jaucourt, Etienne Bonnot de Condillac consigns the state of loafing to the lowest level of inactivity, where idlers wallow in the company of beggars and other wretches. Their idleness consists of perverting necessity—the necessity of *doing*.[7]

The unoccupied individual is portrayed no more reassuringly in the medical writings of the day. The inactive subject may fall prey to a whole series of illnesses: gout, stones, melancholy, madness and, the *Encyclopédie* adds dramatically, "the despair of wasted time" ("Oisiveté," p. 446). The proposed remedy for idleness is work, the discipline of exercise which makes it possible to restore health. The disease of laziness poses a threat to culture through its decadent effeminization, its unmanning effect. This is a far cry from Hercules, the robust hero of labor.

The American Enlightenment was to embrace without reserve this idea of active application. Benjamin Franklin, shored up by the principles of what Max Weber has identified as the "Protestant ethic," elevates industry as a cardinal virtue.[8] He thus condemns its negation, depicting idleness in the most caricatural terms. In his maxims for the self-made man of the market economy, published in *Poor Richard's Almanack* and promptly translated into French under the title *La Science du Bonhomme Richard*, idleness is the diametric opposite of the productive maximization of time. Franklin can admit leisure as compatible with utility only if the former is recuperated by the latter: "Leisure, is Time for doing something useful; this Leisure the diligent man will obtain, but the lazy Man never."[9] In Franklin's view, work must aim to eradicate wasted time. Laziness leads to vice, to abject lethargy, and in the end it depletes life: "Trouble springs from Idleness, and grievous Toil from needless Ease" (p. 490). Franklin charges forth under the banner of

Business, of sovereign *Labor* as compulsive imperative. His worker reduces the time he devotes to sleep and rises at the crack of dawn for the sheer joy of resuming his activity, his industrious rhythm.

In *Discipline and Punish,* Michel Foucault offers a telling perspective on the repression of the idle in the eighteenth century. He provides an explicitly political context for the prohibition of laziness, for its condemnation as the root of the city's evils at the dawn of European industrialization. Foucault goes beyond a simple archaeology of work to study the dialectic of work and idleness, its role in the affairs of State, by means of what he calls a "political technology of the body," a "political anatomy."[10] He explores the way in which the body is invested with power, marked, trained, charged with signifying—in short, subjugated and inserted within a political field:

> This political investment of the body is bound up, in accordance with complex reciprocal relations, with its economic use; it is largely as a force of production that the body is invested with relations of power and domination; but, on the other hand, its constitution as labor power is possible only if it is caught up in a system of subjection (in which need is also a political instrument meticulously prepared, calculated and used); the body becomes a useful force only if it is both a productive body and a subjected body. (*Discipline*, pp. 25–26)

This technology of the body developed by the Ancien Régime is based above all on the mechanisms of production. The useful body par excellence is that of the laborer attached to the machine of production: the instrument-body or machine-body; the menacing obverse of this body is the idle individual, who is incompatible with the norms of production. In *Discipline and Punish,* the theater of industry (to echo the phrase Anthony Vidler applied to Claude-Nicolas Ledoux's saltworks)[11] is the workshop and then the factory, all the sites where the forces of labor become concentrated and where infractions against production and its maximization can be contained.

In the panoply of punishments invented by the eighteenth century, work is conceived as one of the penalties used to combat laziness and vagrancy. A crime against utility must be corrected, forcing the adoption of another attitude. The detention of the idle during the Enlightenment is in fact a pedagogical application of work. Forced labor aims to rehabilitate the lazy subject by integrating him into a project of economic reconstruction and personal reform, bringing to bear the maxim "he who wants to live must work" (*Discipline*, p. 122). Foucault cites Jean-Jacques-Philippe Vilain, a contemporary legislator: "The man who does not find his subsistence must be made to desire to procure it for himself by work; he is offered it by supervision and discipline; in a sense, he is forced to acquire it; he is then tempted by the bait of gain" (*Discipline*, p. 122).

The economist Anne-Robert-Jacques Turgot expresses similar concerns. For him, the administration of the State consists essentially of preventing idleness and indolence. In his *Encyclopédie* article "Fondation," he contrasts "industrious citizens" on one hand with the "vile population" of beggars, vagabonds, and the lazy on the other.[12] For Turgot, industry is the driving force of the State. The ideal administration of the State would consist in achieving full employment, the sole condition for the nation's well-being and wealth. At the time of the Revolution, the Duc de La Rochefoucauld-Liancourt developed similar considerations in his recommendations to the Comité de mendicité (Committee on Begging), created to eradicate a number of social pathologies: begging, poverty, and vagrancy. But what was to come out of the committee's efforts was a new *ethos* of work: "Society owes to all of its members subsistence or work. Whoever is able to work and refuses to do so is guilty of a crime against society and thus loses all right to subsistence."[13] The agents of the State do not hesitate to apply strong measures to repress those who shirk their duty to work. Such behavior constitutes a serious breach of the social contract and places the nation in jeopardy. The pauper who turns down work is perceived as antisocial. The State places these words in the mouth of the offender: "'I wish to remain idle; give me gratis a portion of your property; work for me'—an antisocial proposition in all respects; for whoever consumes and does not produce absorbs the subsistence of the useful man; for the wealth of an empire, existing only in its products, has its origin in the number of its industrious citizens."[14]

In 1789, when Abbé Sieyès formulated the revolutionary idea of the nation in his treatise *Qu'est ce que le Tiers-État?* (*What Is the Third Estate?*), calling for an end to the special privileges of the aristocracy, he placed all citizens under a common obligation, that of work. For this pamphleteer, it is industry that ensures the prosperity of the State. The driving forces behind the nation are production and consumption. Citizens are first and foremost "useful and industrious."[15] The nobility, condemned for its "indolence" (fainéantise; p. 40), must be banished from the shared social project. According to Sieyès, the nobles are out of step with "the general movement"; they are "foreign to the nation" (*Third Estate*, pp. 57–58). They are relegated to the same category as tramps and beggars and "cannot be charged with the political confidence of nations" (*Third Estate*, p. 74).

In her book *Le Travail, reflet des cultures*, Annie Jacob shows how, starting in the mid-seventeenth century, the valorization of labor evolved in the emerging discourse of political economy.[16] If she sees a consensus among various authors regarding the state as the provider of work, a necessary condition for individuals to be useful, she also shows how labor begins to be appreciated as a condition of wealth. But this step was definitively taken only with the advent of the physiocrats. To illustrate this social positivity of work, Jacob points in particular to the work of the Marquis de Mirabeau. And in the face of the physiocrats, represented above all by Quesnay, she examines the writings of a certain Graslin who, even while espousing the ideal of work as a source of wealth, also advanced "socialist" arguments about the inequalities caused by the accumulation of wealth.

The *philosophes*, it must be said, rallied behind the valorization of work and the concomitant moralistic enterprise. Rousseau, in his "Discours sur l'économie politique" ("Discourse on Political Economy"), readily admits the inevitability of work. In considering the responsibilities of government and the commonwealth of the citizens, the philosophe from Geneva declares it essential that work be "always necessary and never useless."[17] Voltaire too sums up the industrious spirit of the century when, scorning idleness as death itself, he proclaims: "to work is to live."[18] One hardly need mention the injunction that the same author places in the mouth of Candide: "we must cultivate our garden."[19] He elaborates on this moral principle: "work keeps away three great evils: boredom, vice, and need" (*Candide*, p. 100). And in his 1734 *Lettres philosophiques*, already rebelling against Pascal's notion of repose, against an original laziness, Voltaire holds action to be a universal law of nature: "Man is made for action, just as fire rises and stones fall"[20]—thus imposing the determinism of utility. Denis Diderot expresses himself in similar terms; commenting on Seneca's writings in his *Essai sur les règnes de Claude et de Néron*, he underlines the dilemma of the idle man, living outside of real time; the solution he proposes is work, replacing a life of indolence with one of action:

> He drags himself miserably from the time he gets up to the time he goes to bed; boredom endlessly prolongs this interval of twelve to fifteen hours, which he counts minute by minute: from days of boredom to more days of boredom, has he reached the end of the year? It seems to him that the first of January blurs immediately into the last day of December, because this whole stretch of time is uninterrupted by any punctuating action. Let's get to work, then: among the advantages of work is that it shortens the days and lengthens life.

Diderot's conclusion: "Better to wear out than to rust."[21]

Finally, late in the century, Immanuel Kant adopts similar language. He considers laziness to be among the most despicable of vices. Its only justification is as a necessary precondition for work, for which it becomes an enjoyable sanction.[22] In the famous essay "What Is Enlightenment?" where Kant proclaims his rallying cry for the century—"*Sapere Aude!* Have courage to use your own reason!"[23]—he immediately associates laziness with cowardice, the condition par excellence of what the philosopher calls the state of tutelage. Laziness represents the primary obstacle to a life of autonomy. Reform by Enlightenment thus requires mental labor. Laziness as passivity is the state from which any exercise of reason takes on an aspect of "irksome work," becoming an "arduous" task. To this state, Kant will oppose a new active posture: walking with the liberated step that must free the subject from the "fetters" or crutches that prevented him from proceeding with confidence ("What Is Enlightenment," pp. 85–86). Access to Enlightenment, like the conquest of liberty, is itself *action* above all.

But it is impossible to neglect the darker, more sordid side of labor in the eighteenth century, the exploitation and slavery associated with the economic consolidation of European imperial powers. Laziness is a priori projected onto the slave as an innate defect—the better to exploit his manpower. The crime of laziness stalks him constantly. In an anonymous brochure published in 1797, *De la nécessité d'adopter l'esclavage en France* (*On the Necessity of Adopting Slavery in France*), the Black is paradoxically judged to be inherently lazy, inimical to laborious activity (black nations are strangers to industry), but at the same time predisposed to work on the plantation, because of his natural tolerance for heat and other local conditions: he is able to "withstand without harm the fatigue exacted by the production of sugar, indigo, and other colonial commodities."[24]

Even abolitionist discourse does not escape the question of preventing laziness. When Commissioner Léger-Félicité Sonthonax proclaims the emancipation of the slaves in Saint-Domingue, abolishes the *Code Noir*,[25] and seeks to establish "a new order of things," he nevertheless takes care to emphasize that the new state of freedom does not exclude labor; on the contrary, he admonishes, "Do not however believe that the liberty you will enjoy will be a state of laziness and leisure. In France, everyone is free, and everyone works; in Saint-Domingue, you are subject to the same laws and will follow the same example."[26] The only change of regime he envisions is in the manner of discipline (the whip is banished) and in the workers' remuneration for the toil demanded of them.

In this context, a noteworthy case is that of Nicolas-Germain Léonard (1744–1793), the writer born in Guadeloupe. He holds a place in literary history as the poet of laziness, as if that were a nostalgic vestige of his origins in the Antilles.[27] Nothing of the kind is true, however: rather, his laziness and his penchant for rest reflect themes borrowed from the classical pastoral imaginary. Léonard follows in the tradition of Fontenelle, adopting the model of the eclogue: Virgilian indolence grazing in the meadows of pastoral Antiquity. However, the reality of colonial slavery does not escape his notice. In his *Lettre sur un voyage aux Antilles* (*Letter on a Voyage to the Antilles*), he describes his return to Guadeloupe, recounting his rounds through various colonial plantations and visits to the estates of colonial administrators. The plantations are bucolic sites of gardens and exotic species of trees which invite the traveler to rest. As for colonial commodities (sugar cane and coffee), they are detached from their reality to become objects of poetic contemplation: "sheaves of light-green canes," "coffee bushes with their bunches of fiery-red berries."[28] Léonard is not blind to the hardship of the slaves' labor, but for the most part he transforms it into rhythm and cadence: he sees the fatigue of labor lifted from the Blacks by their singing and dancing. He often takes a paternalistic attitude toward slavery, never giving a thought to abolition but rather envisioning a system to improve the output and exploitation of the slaves, a deliberate policy for managing population and births among the "creole negroes," which would free the colonies from the transatlantic slave trade (Léonard, pp. 198–200).

The Prosperity of Laziness

This book is thus an invitation to examine the flip side of the eighteenth century. I propose to show, instead of the values of industry, and in the face of the new battle cry for work, individual instances maintaining their distance from the period's prevailing trends. In contrast, at the threshold of industrialization, we find a series of characters set against the grain of utility and functionality, repeatedly contesting the universality of labor and activity. This book explores the margins of normalization, without the usual stigmata of damnation and infamy.

In the following chapters, I will reconstitute an *other* discourse of laziness, a contradictory and oppositional vision that defies what Foucault might call the techno-disciplinary model of mercantile society. My aim is not to compile a history of laziness, but to offer a partial narrative through fragments of an antithetical discourse. Through a number of portraits of *homo otiosus*, mined from the underside of the laborious eighteenth century, various figures of idleness as a positive value will come to light: the journalist of Marivaux's youthful writings and his philosopher bum, Rousseau as a writer belatedly proclaiming laziness in his final years, and Diderot's famous parasite, Rameau's Nephew; but there is also the painter Chardin, the musician Jean-François Rameau, and, at the turn of the next century, the little-known Joseph Joubert.

I have intentionally avoided the aristocrat whose privileged idleness is his virtual birthright. This character, and satires thereof, is found throughout the century (with the most virulent expressions found at the time of the Revolution). A caricatural example is found in a comedy by Monsieur de Launay, *Le Paresseux* (1731). The hero of the play, Damon, is presented as paralyzed by the privileges of his class. His immobile lethargy rests upon his social status and his dwindling fortune. Damon embodies the passion for indolence as an inalienable inheritance. Huddled in his dressing gown, passively managing his possessions, Damon could be the ancestor of the following century's Oblomov, the creation of the Russian writer Ivan Goncharov. In the same vein, one might also point to Xavier de Maistre's somewhat later text, *Voyage autour de ma chambre* (*Voyage Around My Room*, 1795), in which the author describes the insolent and voluptuous *otium* of someone who has capriciously chosen immobility. His "voyage" is also a summons, an invitation to fellow idlers. This proposal of immobility is the effort to end all others: "Buck up, then; we're on our way. . . . let all the lazy people of the world rise *en masse*."[29] The idea is to zigzag aimlessly, frittering away the time. The text is an insistent exercise in meandering, a methodless pursuit of slowness through the room of laziness with its oblique, haphazard topography, "lengthwise and breadthwise, and diagonally too," avoiding the "straight line" (p. 8). Ironically crowning a whole century of travel narratives, de Maistre inverts his own and anchors it within a padded interior. His narrator pursues procrastination in all its guises. The bed becomes a shell dedicated to pleasure, a consummate spot of bliss: "I must admit that I love to savor those sweet moments, and I always prolong as much as possible the pleasure of meditating in the sweet warmth of my bed" (p. 10). This precious bed is conceived as an "ever-changing theater" embracing the various ages of life: the promise of birth, the passing delights of love, but also the final repose of the tomb (p. 10). Other pieces of furniture complement this cozy den of leisure, such as the armchair in which the narrator sinks for a spell of contemplation: "During those long winter evenings, it is often sweet and always advisable to stretch out luxuriously in one, far from the din of the crowds. A good fire, a few books, some quills—what excellent antidotes to boredom!" (p. 9). For the occasion de Maistre's character snuggles in his dressing gown, the traveling costume that swaddles him in his private corner: "My winter traveling coat is made of the warmest, most luxurious fabric I could find: it covers me whole, from head to toe" (p. 72). The narrative of this dilatory voyage consists of putting off for as long as possible the burdensome return to *negotium*, to the "yoke of worldly matters" (pp. 81–82).

Despite such eloquent examples, the laziness arising from the contradictions of bourgeois modernization offers a more intriguing subject of exploration. This laziness takes on a far-reaching signification as soon as the term is detached from the ethical and religious context to which it was originally tied. It can even come full circle to signify its opposite, the paradox of a turbulent, hyper-agitated laziness. The subjects of this book thus anticipate the characters that would emerge in the following century in resistance to the industrial revolution with its capitalist economic order: these include Baudelaire's flâneur and dandy, Rimbaud's Bohemian and vagabond. But their predecessors retain a distinctly eighteenth-century quality.

For Marivaux, laziness resides less in a figure than in a quality of writing practiced by the hero of his journalistic writings, an original embodiment of the philosopher. But laziness is a way for Marivaux to reject the work of abstraction. It is associated with circumstantial, inconsequential reflection. The poetics of laziness cultivates a new form of time: not regular, methodical, linear, but rather unpredictable. Laziness is in tune with transitory time. Marivaux gives us the first elements of this poetics in his composition of a man on the margins, a hero of imprecision and alternation. He sketches the outlines of a truly modern aesthetics of laziness, removed from the models of classical contemplation.

One might imagine the lazy man as bogged down, trammeled by lethargy (as depicted in the critical view of moralistic discourse). But the one I celebrate, on the contrary, is a levitationist. He is buoyed up by the air; his genius unfolds in the fluid element. Chardin captures this spirit perfectly in some of his playful paintings. He places figures in light moments of distraction or detachment, poised within a bubble of leisure, of vaporous atmosphere. In Chardin's work, laziness is liquefied in paint.

The chapters on Diderot and Rousseau will unsettle the attitudes expressed by the philosophes, as recalled above. Here the lazy man emerges as a subject liberated from all constraints. He embraces the creative time of the ephemeral and the circumstantial. The marginality of Diderot's and Rousseau's characters (like Rousseau's literary construction of himself as lazy subject) avenges the individual condemned by state institutions as criminal. Laziness becomes an art of living, an aesthetics of existence, an *attitude* (in the sense of "voluntary choice" that Michel Foucault gives this term in defining modernity),[30] an ingenious appropriation of the moment-to-moment—the insolent and ironic negation of "doing nothing," a paradoxical affirmation of the self in non-acting and non-productivity. Rousseau's lazy man is no longer a citizen constrained by law, but rather a free agent.

I am guided in my undertaking by the original distinction between labor and work that is proposed by Hannah Arendt in *The Human Condition*.[31] For Arendt, work is separate from the universe of hardship; it is an enchanted spell that suspends labor through art and creativity. This book on worklessness takes that dialectic even further. It revalorizes leisure by making the negation or suspension of labor a persistent gesture of creation as well. Here non-productivity remains a precious art, a protest against the bourgeois consensus of utility, an original conquest of freedom. In the end, laziness rejoins the essay, the work in progress with no guarantee of completion. It contemplates the unfinished—work interrupted, fragmented without regret.

Idle-ology

Throughout the book, a theoretical discourse will be brought to bear on the literary texts under examination, augmenting this other vision of laziness. First, there is Michel Foucault, quoted earlier, who sheds light on Enlightenment discipline and exposes

its bodies chained by techno-production, controlled by the institutions of confinement (hospital, factory, prison). Turning away
from the archeology of those bodies, I write the page of resistance
inspired by Foucault.[32] The idlers of this book are in the first instance individuals resistant to discipline, to the mechanical order:
here they are returned to their nomadic potentiality. At various
points I invoke also philosophers such as Gilles Deleuze and Michel Serres, who represent what I would call a post-modernist current in opposition to the Enlightenment. When I conjure up a volatile and fluid world in opposition to that of solids, I have in mind
Serres's re-envisioning of physics on the basis of chaos theory. This
anti-Cartesian philosopher par excellence rejects the methodical
and linear in favor of the *randonnée*, the rambling irregularity of
the random. Serres's preferred geography is uneven, unpredictable.
His approach rejects both system and domination. In his *Éloge de
la philosophie en langue française*, he criticizes the scientific univer-
salism of the Enlightenment; for him it is Rousseau who redeems
the century. In Serres's view, Rousseau refuses abstract geometry
and method, proposing instead the promenade as a way of visiting
"idle and lazy" nature.[33] Rousseau collects plants, attunes himself
to the sites he discovers, indulges in convoluted detours through
the aleatory and the serendipitous: "Jean-Jacques's way of rambling visits every spot on the island [of Saint-Pierre] and allows all
its plants and flowers to flourish" (p. 144). Serres also directs his
criticism at Laplace's work in astronomy, which married Newton's
physics (with its law of central forces, the simple law of attraction)
to that of Descartes (with its whirlwinds). This amalgam produces
a remarkable system of equilibria and calculable parameters, a
planetary vision that neutralizes anomalies and aberrations. Lapla-
cian astronomy globalizes space through abstraction and eliminates obstacles, rationalizing the planetary system.

Serres's countercurrent to this abstraction shares an affinity
with Gilles Deleuze and Félix Guattari. Here I invoke their phi-

losophy of "itineration," the term by which they designate the scientific approach that privileges the model of ambulation, of mobility.[34] Itineration chooses variation over constancy. Another key concept is the rhizome, which tends to decenter by displacement and ramification, in contrast to the tree which fixes and immobilizes. Deleuze and Guattari also favor multiplicity over unity, fragmentation over uniformity. Their geography leaves room for discontinuities; it refuses totalization and linearity. The Cartesian *cogito* is contested for conceiving of space as calculable only from "one point to another" (p. 377). By contrast, Deleuzian nomadology, as a philosophy of fluid and ambulatory processes, of heterogeneous varieties, is turbulent, swirling. It deviates from the gravity of Newtonian physics, in favor of an alternative model that is heterogeneous, differentiated, multiple. In *A Thousand Plateaus*, the science of attraction is the very model of legal science: attraction is the "law of all laws" (p. 370). Deleuze and Guattari point to its pretention of universality, based exclusively on a postulate of constancy and homogeneity. Weight is "a constant relation for all variables" (p. 370). Yet the space of attraction is actually contradicted by other models of space, of eddying flows, operating through separation and speed and escaping the model of gravity.[35] When Deleuze and Guattari consider the notion of work, they refer to the mechanistic physical model, the scientific conception of work with its constant quantitative value. To this notion they oppose that of "free action" as a mobile, non-quantifiable force that is impossible to subjugate: "In free action, what counts is the way in which the elements of the body escape gravitation to occupy absolutely a nonpunctuated space" (p. 397).[36]

These discourses will intersect throughout the book as laziness serves to open up an *other* vision of the eighteenth century. If the narratives I have chosen are distanced from a universalist vision of work, there is an even more profound detachment from the Enlightenment as an ideology of totalization, as the only path of rationality. The fleeting observations of Marivaux's Spectator, Chardin's distraction, Rousseau's promenade, Rameau's vagrancy, and Joubert's laziness, all nomadic and disengaged activities, embrace a project of slowing down while proclaiming a new order of liberties.

[1]

The Surprises of Laziness

Marivaux

Laziness is not a trait that is usually associated with Pierre Carlet de Marivaux, prolix playwright and innovative novelist that he was. Nevertheless, in certain autobiographical fragments and a number of his other writings, laziness remains a persistent preoccupation. Despite his rich dramatic output and his success in various comical genres that were popular at the time, Marivaux repeatedly mentions laziness as a private dream. In fact, Marivaux's laziness is intimately linked to writing, to its constant renegotiation of the future. I would thus like to examine other texts upon which Marivaux leaves a special stamp, a particularly modern quality of writing. What interests me here is Marivaux as a journalist, in writings that could well be described as youthful efforts, produced in the interval between his dramatic publications and his law degree. In 1721, Marivaux tries his hand at a genre imported from England: he creates for his compatriots a French version of *The Spectator*, the periodical launched by Joseph Addison and Richard Steele in the first decade of the century. This work is part of a resolutely modern aesthetic project that represents an ideological break with the *anciens*: an attempt to put the present into prose. It will become apparent that the modernity broached by Marivaux is not confined to the aesthetic sphere; it is clearly epistemological. Marivaux's periodical inaugurates a model of philosophical writing in which the author separates himself from Cartesian thought and its mechanical physics. At the dawn of the Enlightenment, proclaiming his modernity, Marivaux refuses systematic and methodical rationality; he proposes instead a sensory *cogito*, attentive to the real and subjected to the aleatory, a physics of liquid elements. The laziness that I evoke in this book embodies this philosophical initiative.

In *Le Spectateur français*, Marivaux is a painter of modern life, of "the world as it is." We shall see that in his own way, Marivaux anticipates Baudelaire's definition of modernity as "the transitory, the fleeting, the contingent."[1] As proposed by Marivaux, laziness loses any claim of transcendence. His attitude of solitary contemplation without philosophical depth is a reaction to the urban environment. Later, in the context of the Indigent Philosopher, we shall see this nuance more finely drawn, when Marivaux describes his character as "the man without a care." Couched within this phrase is an allusion to Christian *acedia*, a form of apathy that monastics may experience. But Marivaux's negligence is easily liberated from this context. This same laziness devoid of moral gravity is what allows Marivaux's narrators to pick and choose from the present, from the daily offering. Such laziness is all the more capricious in that it finds itself confronted with what Walter Benjamin saw as "the essential interminability that distinguishes the preferred obligations of the idler."[2]

Marivaux quickly diverges from his English predecessors, not only by giving his publication a personal dimension but especially by gallicizing the English model. *Le Spectateur français* takes its place within the essayistic tradition of Montaigne,[3] Pascal, and La Bruyère, authors who were to remain models of style and originality for Marivaux.

Who is this Spectator, this polygraph of everyday life? From the start, as I have said, Marivaux seeks to invent a new kind of writing. The moralist of the everyday wants to avoid any authorial gravity, any thinking that involves work. Instead the Spectator, the scribe of circumstance, holds himself in readiness for events as they transpire. Marivaux insists that this openness to the incidental is the total absence of work, the opposite of the artificial exercise of the mind:

An author is a man who, in his leisure moments, is over-taken by a vague desire to think about one or several sub-jects; and one might call this reflecting upon nothing. This type of work has often produced excellent results for me, I admit; but ordinarily what one experiences here is more an elasticity of mind than any naturalness and truth; in any case it is true that the thoughts are connected by some sort of artificial taste that one finds exciting. For after all the choice of these thoughts is purely arbitrary, and that is what it means to reflect as an author.[4]

As for the Spectator, he abandons himself to the "randomness of things" (p. 114). He lets the occasion come to him. If authorial reflection "tortures" thought, fetters the spirit with an arbitrary chain of ideas, by contrast the Spectator's thought is the fruit of the event that it embraces. It places itself at the disposal of the oc-casion: "I know only how to surprise in myself the thoughts that chance presents, and I would be hard put to add anything of my own. . . . My intent is to think neither well nor badly, but simply to capture faithfully what comes to me from following the course of imagination laid out by the things that I see or hear" (p. 114). The results are not concepts that tire the mind but rather, to use Michel Gilot's expression, "objects of sentiment."[5]

The Spectator is in his element outdoors. He is actually a product of the object; it is the event that situates him. The Specta-tor is the guest, the devoted disciple, of circumstance. He seeks another mind, an imagination that he claims "would indeed be worth every bit as much as that born of work and attention" (p. 115). Marivaux gives a name to these objects, these occasions for lightweight thought: he calls them "trifles" (bagatelles; p. 138). The supple imagination slips readily from the weighty to the frivolous, from the serious to the laughable. What is essential is the meet-ing of thought and happenstance, the primacy of the object. In his journals, Marivaux adheres to the letter of the expression: "matter for reflection" or, as he says in his own terms, "matter of reflection" (p. 117). The object is what "exercises" (p. 117) the imagination, what sets it in motion, what propels and generates writing.

Marivaux plays with the distinction between *ratio* and *intellectus*, in the sense recalled by Josef Pieper. *Ratio* belongs to the sphere of discursive thought and abstraction, whereas *intellectus* belongs to seeing: vision organizes the world as a landscape to be known. The domain of the intellectus is the absence of work or leisure.[6] This distinction enables us to read the Spectator's idleness as a recasting of classical philosophical contemplation.[7] This is the status of the observer in the modern city, amid the urban vortex. The Spectator is the "contemplator of human things" (p. 142). Indeed, he lives only "in order to see and to hear" (p. 117).[8] His perspective on the world is therefore *theoretical* (in the etymological sense of seeing, of attachment to observation and contemplation), requiring a new mode of contact with reality, a mode that runs against the grain of activity, the confused bustle of the *polis*. The observer's mind is always *situational* (p. 127). Marivaux frames the newly prestigious status of the journalist's life in this quest for truth. He inscribes it within a new hierarchy of thought.

One might also think of the narrator of *La Vie de Marianne*. The "chatterbox" (babillarde)[9] of the novel has the same goals as those of the Spectator. She refuses to write a book proper; rather, her writing is modeled after conversation. She is continually digressing and ruminating, rejecting the obligatory sequential narrative: "I would become hopelessly bogged down by the mental effort required" (*Vie de Marianne*, p. 71). Marianne prefers to find her own way. She babbles away, indulging in bantering reflection, in a morality arising out of occasion and circumstance, out of events. She chalks reflection up to "sentiment" which, unlike the mind, does not concoct ideas "to suit itself" (*Vie de Marianne*, p. 60). But above all, Marianne also writes against a natural inclination, laziness, which she sets aside in order to "scribble over a lot of paper": "I am going to tell you a story that will be quite long . . .

but I do not wish to think of that, my laziness must not find out: let us press onward!" (*Vie de Marianne*, p. 56).

(Anti-)treatise on the Volatile

The *feuille volante* or loose leaf is the ideal tool for the Spectator.[10] In one issue of *Le Spectateur*, we find the word *volatile*, a term that beautifully expresses the ideal of the leaf wafted about at the whim of the wind.[11] It calls for brevity and lightness, for the furtive anecdote and the ephemeral. His eyes peeled and ears cocked, Marivaux creates a dream, the portrait of a coquette, the adventure of an Unknown woman. He slips in a moral reflection, the fragmentary Journal of a Spaniard, epistolary exchanges. The Spectator savors these brief morsels: short parables, sketches for a novel. D'Alembert, in his "Éloge de Marivaux," summed up the Spectator's kaleidoscope of snapshots, the variety presented by Marivaux's vignettes: "In a variety of images, often humorous and genial, he paints the machinations of ambition, the torments of greed, the treachery or cowardice of friends, the ungratefulness of children and the injustice of fathers, the insolence of the rich, the tyranny of protectors."[12] But Marivaux introduced an important modulation to his notion of the *tableau*: "we are all vignettes in one another's eyes" (p. 134), he writes in *Le Spectateur*. He captures individuals *in relation*, situated face to face, reciprocally viewed as spectacles of one another[13]—hence the insistence in his journal on circumstantial postures and masks. *Le Spectateur* is thus a garden of assorted physiognomies.

Once again, the writer distances himself from forced research, from the work of abstraction: "Yes, I would prefer all the fortuitous ideas that chance confers, over those that the most ingenious efforts could achieve through work" (p. 117). Here we find an interesting distinction: the author's idleness that Marivaux finds engrossing and futile, that mires the author in cumbersome,

artificial, arduous thought, is to be contrasted with the ease preferred by the Spectator, the journalist's "insurmountable laziness"
(p. 117), which fosters a sort of abandon, a moral lightness and
aimlessness. The leisure to which the journalist dedicates himself
is fluid and unconstrained. It is open to the multiplication of possibilities, in search of "novelties" (p. 134). The serendipitous idea
abhors depth. At any moment Marivaux may stop short, laying
down his feather pen; as he says: "I feel that I am being weighed
down" (p. 137). Above all, the writer is not tied to any formula.
He chooses what comes easily to hand. The luxury of observation
is the "libertinage of ideas" that spurns the "fixed subject" (p. 132)
and enables the journalist to keep deferring, to put off until another time whatever he doesn't feel like developing at a given moment. He interrupts and resumes his observations at the whim of
his laziness (p. 252) or, on the contrary, because "doing nothing"
(p. 253) bores him.

Already in his *Lettres sur les habitants de Paris*, Marivaux's narrator adopted this same capricious strategy, the same libertinage:
"I continue randomly, and I stop when I feel like it. This work is,
in a word, the product of a libertine mind, which rejects nothing
amusing along its path" (*Journaux*, p. 8). The chronicle becomes a
text of bifurcations; the multiple stories follow one upon another
propelled by interruptions and chance meetings, "in circuitous by-
ways" (p. 127), "going down the stairs of the Comédie" (p. 123),
"in a public plaza" (p. 166). Communication is constantly subject
to interference; the text burgeons, branches out. By deferring and
postponing, the narrator assumes his place within the realm of
time. He thus simulates time as a detachable sequence of discrete
rather than successive, causal, or rational moments. Life itself is
pictured as a relay of episodes. One must also keep in mind the
erratic publication rhythm of the periodical, punctuated by fre-
quent and lengthy interruptions, subjected to the journalist's passing fancy, his mood, his laziness. He offers countless accidents and
diverse circumstances to justify the delays.

The Spectator reserves his harshest words for the critics who end up writing according to the dictates of their censors. Base imposters, wretched copyists, "they chase after wit" (p. 146)—a reversal of the accusation leveled against Marivaux himself. What is the alternative? Free, relaxed thought that keeps its own "rhythm" (p. 147), "obeys its own fire" (p. 145). Servility and philosophical subjection make up the antibody of the Marivaudian observer's enterprise: his thought is simple. The Spectator "goes his own merry way" (p. 147). Liberty, naturalness, or, to use Marivaux's own term, "naïveté" are also a quest for absolute singularity, for the sovereignty of one's own style. The point is "never to depart from the course or character of ideas for which nature has given us a calling; in a word, to retain the singularity of mind that has been granted us" (p. 149). The feeling Marivaux describes, which he calls the nerve center of "spectatorial" writing, is that singularity of affect, a moral declaration risked *for the pleasure of it*, offered gratuitously, for what it is worth, on the spur of the moment. The Spectator's morality is always on the edge of "humor" (plaisanterie; p. 126). The key is never to be "dogmatic" (p. 236). The observer insists that he writes above all for his own pleasure: "ideas occur to me; they give me pleasure" (p. 245).

The observer cultivates the instructive promenade, the *flânerie* ever full of surprises. He likes the profusion of occasions, the thronging of events. For this reason his theater is the street, the *basso continuo* or background against which discrete snapshots stand out. The street represents the out-of-bounds, an extraterritoriality, the uncertain space that brings individuals together; a site of unexpected encounters, it is the place where chance interactions, the collision of individualities and eccentric images, give rise to meaning:

I wanted to run through the world's teeming streets; what a delectable feast the spectacle of such a large number of people gathered together offers to a misanthrope—the time to harvest his ideas. This infinite quantity of varied movements coalesces to form a generic character in his eyes. In the end, so many subjects are reduced to a single one; no longer is he contemplating distinct men, but rather man represented in several thousand men. (p. 133)

This explains the particular expression that the Spectator uses to illustrate his mode of reflection, his refusal of abstraction, his occasional thought. He wishes he himself could "think as *men*" (p. 114; emphasis added). The journalist once again chooses the multiplicity, diversity, and moral variegation of the species. He embraces a plural subjectivity in the face of ephemeral existential situations, which make sense only in the fleeting instant.

The Spectator pursues the mob in its motley abundance. Like the bee, he is drawn to commotion, to the perpetual appeal of the swarm: "My curiosity satisfied, I withdrew to gather nectar elsewhere" (p. 134). He chases after diversity of observation: "I like to change subjects" (p. 206). The same predilection for the multiple, the precedence of multitude and heterogeneity, are what guide Marivaux in his moral observations. His epistemological interest in crowds, "this horde of the world" (p. 126), the manifold swirl, is another sign of Marivaux's modernity—another anticipation of that other Painter of modern life, whose own *flâneur* wishes to "commingle with the mob": "what an immense pleasure it is to take up residence in number, in the whirl of movement, in the fleeting and the infinite," proposed Baudelaire,[14] another modern spectator whose chosen habitat was the out-of-doors.

In the "Sixième feuille," Marivaux stages a representation of his own book. In a bookseller's shop, a man in search of serious reading is proposed a copy of *Le Spectateur*; the man expresses his bias against these "leaves." In his view, this type of writing, these "short works," betray a frivolous mind, a lack of depth: "can reason, good sense, and subtlety be found in such a small quantity of paper? . . . Has any good mind ever seen fit to think and to write other than in large volumes?" (p. 138). A large tome is seen as worth its weight in reason. But Marivaux counters this argument by defending the buoyant *feuille volante*, ready to be lifted up "with a breath" (p. 138). What the Spectator presents as an anti-model is the *Traité de morale* (*Treatise on Morality*; p. 138), a heavy brick of a book ready to preach on the strength of its weight alone: "it is morality, and single-minded, unadulterated morality" (p. 139). The conditioned reader, the devotee of "weight" and seriousness, is also judged severely: "what he seeks is not so much usefulness as the honor of acting as a man capable of exerting himself to find this usefulness, and the vast desert of a heavy book fits the bill" (p. 139). Marivaux explicitly mentions the "gravity" of the collector of "volumes." If the term refers to character, the physical sense is not far off: he also has in mind the object's weight. The big book that buttresses method and system weighs in on the side of solid bodies, of strength; in contrast, Marivaux's matter is airy and light: breath, fire, heat. I would suggest that it partakes of the physics of fluids (liquids and gases).[15]

In *Liquid Modernity*, Zygmunt Bauman explains the essential difference between solids and liquids. He elucidates how fluid, as a body that is always on the point of change, is the product of time. Fluids are mobile, traveling bodies.[16] Bauman expands: "fluids do not keep to any shape for long and are constantly ready (and prone) to change it; and so for them it is the flow of time that counts, more than the space they happen to occupy: that space, after all, they fill but 'for a moment'" (Bauman, p. 2). The term *volatile*, which also belongs to the field of chemistry, where it describes an evaporated substance, applies quite aptly to the leaf, to vapor, to the ephemeral.[17] In the play between the "*feuille volante*" and the despised "volume" lies another physical opposition. Volume is what takes up space, takes on a consistency, in contrast with the flying, flighty, volatile leaf. Marivaux's term volatile, which favors subtle matter, brilliantly heralds the universe of information, of the event transformed into signs. The Spectator is a messenger: he translates, intercepts, transmits, all at once.[18] The "frivolous"

(p. 134) that the Spectator eagerly takes hold of is the diametric opposite of the solid, the hard. The mind or spirit elected by Marivaux is to be understood in the physical sense as an emanation that is light, liquid, volatile. And when Marivaux praises the sublime, it is a sign of his devotion to the subtle, to the same vaporous element: "warmth of spirit," "the fire of perception."[19]

In *Le Cabinet du philosophe* (*The Philosopher's Study*, 1734), Marivaux returns to the opposition between leaf and volume, and recalls the a priori notions associated with the two types of works:

> The leaf seems to promise a mere trifle. . . . But a volume is respectable. . . . After all to present the public with a volume is to take a very serious tone; it is to say, beware of what you are about to read: which is precisely what one does not say when one offers readers no more than a leaf; it even seems as if one is saying the opposite, and that one is asking them to read as a simple distraction, merely in passing and for lack of anything better to do.[20]

The *feuille* is best read without really taxing one's attention. These leaves of the philosophe are fugitive reflections, written in quasi-secrecy. Any labor must be invisible, no signs of effort must be seen. Such a work turns up as a lucky find, a surprise. Like our Spectator, the philosophe sets himself up "as a student of men" (*Journaux*, p. 335). Whence the brevity of thought, its conversational tone: "It is not a question here of a well-developed work: these are, for the most part, separate pieces, fragments of thought on an infinity of subjects, and in all sorts of styles" (*Journaux*, p. 335). The philosophe too has fashioned himself through multiple, heterogeneous reflection, through variety.

In the "Quinzième feuille" of *Le Spectateur*, Marivaux offers another representation of his book, another *mise en abîme* of his *Spectateur*. He incorporates in his volume a "short notebook" written in Spanish, for which he immediately provides a translation, *Continuation de mon Journal*. The notebook, found buried in a "large volume" (p. 193) purchased at random from an inventory sale, is itself pure serendipity—an unplanned event, a pleasing circumstance, a true find. It represents a minor accident, a lighter element released from a weighty structure. The narrator begins thus: "this morning I opened my window between eleven and noon; the minute I opened it, there was a strong gust of wind; I moved to draw back, for it seemed impossible to stay there: and just imagine, I would have missed a moral lesson" (p. 193). Here again we see the volatile wind-blown work, which Marivaux conflates with moral turbulence and existential instability. Morality itself is buffeted by the wind: the lesson is grasped in the moment, rather than through an artificial abstraction like that of the moral Treatise. Here, as only Marivaux could phrase it, is vanity at the mercy of a gust of wind:

> This wind revealed something to me, it taught me that it places many men in a situation that I had thought indifferent, but which actually causes them grief. Life is full of unhappiness! Alas! I was not unaware that the wind caused many misfortunes, that it destroyed houses, uprooted trees, and flattened crops, not to mention its ravages upon the ocean; I will say nothing of the blinding dust it stirs up . . . these were the only sad effects I was familiar with. But this is far from the whole story; besides all that, it can also distress people personally, wounding their self-esteem. This is how. As I went to close my window, I saw three or four young men whose hair was curled, powdered, arranged with such skill that only a Frenchman could have done it: you would have said that Cupid himself had coiffed that hair with his own hands. . . . Suddenly, the attack begins, and there is trouble; the wind blows and catches them at the left ear. Quickly they duck, writhe, seek out a hundred different postures in aid of this miserable side insulted by the wind. (pp. 193–194)

The Spectator places himself at the heart of the inclement weather. His observation records the jarring of hearts, the discomposure of fellow human beings. Marivaux takes it further: he sends his subjects whirling in a vortex. They scramble pell-mell in innumerable "postures." Thus, Marivaux's tableau is never still but, like a barometer of the occasional, follows the vagaries of time: "What an unhappy state! It moved me, I was upset that I had gone to the window, I was fighting the wind alongside them, but the wind was victorious. . . . Oh! as these young men began to struggle so painfully with the last remaining bit of powder and styling, I could stand it no longer" (p. 194). Later, the observer considers his own vanity: "I thought that the wind would not let up, that a single stroke of bad luck was all that was required to strip me of my powder" (p. 194). Marivaux portrays the random elements vividly: wind, dust, powder, a whole creation consigned to vanishing.[21] He shows the fragile universe, the sudden irruption of disorder. Powder and dust: the narcissistic cloud meets the flurry and turmoil of matter. Marivaux's moral is properly meteorological. As before, in the case of the crowd, here the author makes turbulence, chaos, and circumstance his own.[22]

The metaphoric and epistemic field in which Marivaux writes, as we have seen, privileges the multiple and the corpuscular. In his *Lettres sur les habitants de Paris*, he discovers the genius of the people, a tableau vivant of "opposites."[23] The people of Paris are a restless monster, a moral hodge-podge, a "compound of all good and bad qualities combined" (*Lettres*, p. 10). When describing the fragile bonds that hold the populace together, the miraculous equilibrium of vices and virtues, Marivaux thinks of the ocean's turbulence: "winds and lightning hold constant sway; the ship sails on unawares: storms are familiar to it, lightning sometimes strikes, but it is such a natural outgrowth of the storm that the ship tries to repair itself without a shudder. Setting aside the obsession with etiquette, choppy seas seem to me preferable to calm seas" (*Lettres*, p. 12). To describe the people of Paris, Marivaux chooses images of ocean swells and storms. He uses objects swayed by movement and oscillation to paint the fluid, hydraulic phenomenon of people who form, he says, a "chameleon" (*Lettres*, p. 12), a subtle machine, one susceptible to chance, to accidents of virtue as well as those of vice. The reptilian image is not negative to Marivaux: on the contrary, the changes weathered by the people are the essence of their fecundity. Here again we find the Marivaux of winds and waters, the metaphysician of turbulence and transitory states.

Marivaux's attitude could be described as profoundly anti-Cartesian. Michel Serres observes how the Cartesian text excludes the fluid and the composite: "Cartesian idealism is a form of realism: the things of the world do not disappear into the thinking subject; on the contrary, the subject retreats indefinitely in favor of objects. Physics is grounded. It concerns only solid matter."[24] In his physical intuition more than in his aesthetic affinities, Marivaux can be said to be closer to Pascal. He chooses variation as his model, acknowledging the ascendancy of space and discontinuous topology. Thus, the Spectator rejects deductive reasoning in favor of fluctuating contingency. Rather than adhering to method, he deviates from the beaten path. His is an art of distraction, of abandon and reiteration. It has been accurately observed that Marivaux did not adopt his English predecessors' "meticulous and methodical" mode of thought, or their "esprit de suite" (intellectual consistency).[25] But there are some detours that Marivaux recommends avoiding. These are the ones that weigh down the mind, forcing it to conform to an artificial order. The Spectator thus considers the "contortion" in which the mind "finds its provisions only through onerous labor" (p. 145). He advocates following in nature's footsteps, its "straight path," and avoiding whatever opposes liberty of mind, such as "an assumed step that diverts him from his paths and sends him down sterile roads, continually cut off" (p. 145). *Le Spectateur* can only be an open, pluralistic, multicolored work that switches narrators, incorporating its own real or fictive readers. Redundancy in all its senses is to be avoided, at any cost. The Spectator's motto is "Let us change" (p. 245). The reader's expectations must be altered by changes of narrative: "As I have become accustomed to changing subjects on practically every page, some day I will be able to dwell for a long time on the same subject, as just one more form of variety" (p. 206).

The Spectator's day-by-day chronicle is fragmentary and flexible. It takes its cue from time, sometimes from the weather of the moment. In *L'Indigent philosophe* (*The Indigent Philosopher*), Marivaux gives this definition of a "methodical author": "He has a fixed subject to which he will apply himself; well and good: he knuckles down to it, and then he is stuck with it. . . . He has half a dozen thoughts in his head upon which he bases the entire work; they are rooted in one another."[26] By contrast, the realism that Marivaux introduces in *Le Spectateur* favors the sensory, but in the form of scattered information. The Spectator scatters himself. The act of observation seeks the element of surprise. Like a hunter, the journalist chases after spontaneous information. His activity is fortuitous, the product of chance. He exercises his observation not in order to pin down the elements observed; on the contrary, they are abandoned to their random fate, caught up in an emergent process of creation. These ephemeral constellations are not the target of any effort to unify or impose mastery; they are left to develop in their own exteriority.

The various narrators of Marivaux's leaves thus write in the present, transcribing the prose of the instant, celebrating everyday events. As he often does, Marivaux opens *Le Spectateur* to another voice, that of a lady who, in a moment of distraction, allows the narrator to make off with half of a notebook she has written: the words are stolen, lifted in the levity of an opportune moment. If the Spectator perpetrates a theft, he also moves the object into the order of the fleeting, of messages that vanish: the stolen work disintegrates and dissipates of its own accord, virtually volatilized. The Spectator eagerly reproduces his old friend's words and offers us her *Mémoire de ce que j'ai dit et fait pendant ma vie* (*Memoir of What I Have Said and Done in My Life*). The words taken from this other narrator, which open this half of her notebook, might as well belong to the Spectator himself: "I live only in the passing moment; then comes another one that is already gone, which I have lived through, it is true, but in which I no longer am, and it is as if I have never existed. Could I not thus say that my life does not last, that it is constantly beginning?" (pp. 207–208). Marivaux, whose predilection for random, fluctuating time we have seen, celebrates ephemeral time, the day-to-day—the precious succession of instants, the present pregnant with possibilities.

Le Spectateur immediately touched off critiques of what would be called *marivaudage*, Marivaux's preciosity, or at least his loquacious badinage. This very predilection for levity is what I am celebrating here, *contra* the spirit of his earliest critics, who missed the essential. In one of the last issues of *Le Spectateur*, Marivaux revisits yet again his refusal of a certain philosophical method: "Leave it to certain scholars, I mean the system-builders, those popularly known as philosophers—leave it to them to methodically pile up vision upon vision while reasoning on the nature of the two substances, or on similar things" (p. 323). In fact, if Marivaux's metaphysics is never profound, nor erudite, nor dogmatic, it is because he nurtures a fundamental belief that man is impossible to plumb, that he is multifaceted, a very mixed bag: "a wonderful economy of light and dark" (p. 233). For these reasons, the Spectator's morality will always float like a leaf wafted upon the graceful mist of intellect.

The Man without a Care (*The Indigent Philosopher*)

Marivaux will return to his "leaves," but in a new reincarnation, that of a Pauper-philosopher. The narrator has sequestered himself far from France, "more than five hundred leagues away" (p. 275) from his homeland. But like his predecessor the Spectator, he continues to think about Paris as a great theater. In the same vein, he is a flâneur, seeking the inventive spectacle of the outdoors: "I take to the streets to see everybody, I amuse myself with the passersby" (p. 278). The "voluble" (p. 277) narrator writes at his leisure. Marivaux clothes him in a cloak of poverty, as a vagrant philosopher begging for his sustenance. Flouting the reigning ordinances against degenerate good-for-nothings who deprive the state of useful labor,[27] the Pauper parades his glorious destitution: "I am supreme in my poverty, a poor man fit even to be painted, for my clothes are in tatters and the rest of my company follows suit" (p. 276). This is the sovereignty of wretchedness. In defiance of his bad fortune, this beggar practices philosophy: "being poor is not enough. . . . one must know how to turn it to one's advantage" (p. 276).

For Marivaux's character, idleness is not a negative state. It even becomes "time for living" (p. 277). *Far niente* is an opportunity for a unique, discriminating form of asceticism. The absence of labor leads to a work of time as art: "no one will swindle me out of the moments I choose to spend doing nothing: hooray for empty pleasures" (p. 277). Idleness is above all a *style* (p. 278), the art of adaptability: it sparks the genius of circumstance and the instantaneous. The "lie-in" (grasse matinée; p. 278) of the slugabed yields to the conditions of the moment. "Things pass by, and I watch them go," declares the Pauper (p. 307). He is the friend and spectator of happenstance.

The Pauper avoids all situations of subjugation. He is at heart "the man without a care" (l'homme sans souci; p. 281). He criticizes all disciplinary devices, such as etiquette with its manners dictated by "convention," and the straitjacket of self-scrutiny: "one must keep an eye on oneself" (p. 323), he remarks. Likewise, his sidekick in the narrative, his companion in penury—another Pantalon of laziness—flees the military establishment. Unskilled in musketry and disinclined to obedience, he chooses desertion and renounces the occupation of soldier. He explains his refusal of discipline thus: "one must obey a captain with a will of his own, one is better off following one's own desires rather than someone else's" (p. 284). In this spirit, we might think of Marivaux's contemporary Watteau, who, as Arlette Farge has demonstrated, produced a body of anti-militaristic paintings. Watteau is interested in the deserter, the soldier recalcitrant to discipline and drills. In painting the war, he avoids heroic representation and concentrates instead on lethargy, languor, and fatigue. Farge argues that Watteau puts war "out of commission" (en panne),[28] deflating military representation with impromptu moments taken from everyday existence, from harm-less, circumstantial lives. Indeed, Watteau paints a version of the wayward soldier at extreme ease, his weapons in abeyance.

For Marivaux's Pauper, as for the companion to whom he tem-porarily hands over his narrative, happiness is to be found in "a dis-orderly life" (p. 286), woven of chance, lined with circumstance. This life of randomness must be understood as a way to avoid the constraints of time as a sequence of regular, predictable events: "to be warm today and cold tomorrow, guzzle one's drink and wolf down one's food, to work, do nothing, walk the city and the fields, tire oneself out, have good times, pleasure and pain, that is what I needed" (p. 286). In keeping with this interrupted, episodic life, the philosopher's double proffers reflections that are "utterly confused" and proposes reaping the "bits and pieces" (p. 294) that are agree-able. In order to survive, he exploits "all the detours" (p. 285). Like-wise, his story progresses through "parenthesis" (p. 313) and digres-sion. Avoiding orderly narrative, the Pauper's companion is another nomad, an eleventh-hour actor in the theater of "chance" (p. 291), a passe-partout. Stasis and permanence are unthinkable to him.

Alongside his companion, Marivaux's beggar celebrates wine, the magical philter of fellowship, a ferment of communication and connection. At every turn, he raises a toast to the merry bottle: "Let us drink!" is his rallying cry. Wine *simply* humanizes: "when one has wine, anything goes; it makes people good and human" (p. 290). Wine is the medium through which the companion's story passes from the Pauper to us, as an exchange between brothers. From the bottle pours a bottomless stream of narrative. In the end, the Pauper leaves the stage of the book to go share a meal with other beggars, a feast of freedom and unbridled appetite. They eat and drink without the contortions of civility. The two characters part the way they met, by chance. Each returns to the anonymity of the crowd.

Marivaux's Pauper seeks "man" (p. 304); he wants to put truth to the test. He constructs his quest as a veritable philosophical hunt, quickly running through the evil man, the hypocrite, the proud. But of course there are only *men*. No doubt this difficult and ultimately *cynical* research brings him back to himself, to his tranquil asceticism, his light-hearted quietude, his frivolous abandon. The Indigent, anticipating Diderot's Nephew, may be seen as a modern successor to Diogenes. Indeed, Marivaux borrows from the ancient Cynic the same posture of non-productivity, the sovereign choice of poverty, the acceptance of contingency. This new Diogenes, the Indigent, also wears his cloak of misery.[29]

For Marivaux's errant philosopher, freedom leads in the end to a writing strategy in keeping with the existential trace. Indeed, in his *Mémoires*, he adopts a poetics of "disorder" (p. 310), casting aside all rules and methods. The Pauper exemplifies a complex nature, a varied, fractal landscape: "Look at nature, it has plains, then valleys and mountains, here trees, there rocks, no symmetry, no order, I mean the kind of order that we know and that, to my taste, cuts such a silly figure next to nature's beautiful disorder" (p. 311). He practices the unruly contemplation of fantasy, the joyous and liberated exercise of "reason" (p. 279), a simple "morality" (p. 279). His "leaves" and "sheaves of paper" (p. 324) resemble "rhapsodies" (p. 303); his thought prefers "delightful variegation" (p. 310). The word "bigarrure" (variegation; p. 310), a favorite of Marivaux's, conveys the composite assemblage, the kaleidoscopic jumble, the mix of unmatched parts of his willfully "bizarre" (p. 310) work, in the image of nature itself.

Marivaux chooses interesting characters: not consistent subjectivities, but rather subjects susceptible to variation, nomads rebelling against order and rules, their identities in flux. The Pauper, a veritable Harlequin, the patchwork comic hero, is a paragon of such bigarrure, a hodge-podge through and through. The philosopher's clothes "in tatters," his "rags" (p. 276), are the stuff of portraiture. His leaves, like his clothing, are "slovenly shreds" (p. 279). Marivaux uses identical terms to describe both clothing and text, their common materiality. Here again, in the end, we find the Pascalian Marivaux, the man of splintered, sporadic space.[30] The philosopher "in ragged clothes" (p. 281) offers the same heteroclitic portrait. He is "stained" (p. 281). The term conveys not only his ruined state, but also the subject's hybrid qualities; it shows a jumbled, blotched image. The Pauper limps a bit, his gait is halting, his step off balance. He wends his way as best he can, stumbling along his twisted path, his progress muddled and desultory.

Requiem

In his *Lettre sur la paresse*, written in 1740, Marivaux once again confesses his laziness in a nostalgic mode. As he humbly takes stock of his achievements, he recalls his choice of a modest life, removed from the appetite for possessions and wealth, from dizzying aquisitiveness: "Ah! blessed laziness! Tonic indolence! If you had remained my nursemaids, I would likely not have written so many more or less witty nothings, but I would have had more happy days than I have had bearable moments."[31] Repose becomes the supreme good for the mind. It avoids the vicissitudes of material things and makes it possible to remain beyond the reach of commercial troubles. Laziness is the only pleasure that can be counted on, when all possessions are forgotten; it is the ecstatic suspension of expenditure. This "congenial laziness" is evoked in Marivaux's *Éloge de la paresse et du paresseux* (*In Praise of Laziness and of the Lazy*).[32] The art of living serenely keeps the lazy man out of polemics and social violence: "Laziness answers to its own justice; it would have to give up its ease in order to commit injustices, or to prolong them. It is incapable of bringing a suit, or even of backing one. . . . Libels and satires cannot be attributed to laziness" (*Éloge*, p. 456). The *Éloge* is unfinished; laziness overtakes the author, who concludes: "I take pleasure in all of these ideas; but too lazy to write them down, exhausted from having dictated them, I would like some charitable soul to undertake such a project for the good of humanity" (*Éloge*, p. 456). He would gladly hand off this task to someone else.

Marivaux defends this light-hearted renunciation, a stance unconcerned with the accumulation of capital, exempt from stockpiling to solidify the future; it represents the carefree joy of having nothing to lose: "rest does not make you richer than you are, but it does not make you poorer: with it you conserve what you do not increase; for all I know, increase may sometimes end up repaying a virtuous indifference to wealth" (*Éloge*, p. 456). Marivaux's will is of the same ilk. His wish is to leave the earth with the utmost humility. In the twilight of his life, he thinks of the paupers that he praised in his work: "I bequeath sixty pounds to the poor of my parish. I wish to be buried at the least expense and with the least fuss possible" (*Journaux*, p. 552). It is with these beggars, to whom he dedicated the fire of his youthful pen, that he would like to remain, without ceremony.

Marivaux is fond of the weak. He prefers the meek, the disinherited. This makes him inventive, open to circumstance, hospitable, close to the rhythm of invention, adaptable. The simple man is without a care; he has cast off his vanity which, like his erstwhile fortune, he happily leaves to others. He throws himself more readily into the great hubbub of the world. Open to all possibilities, adapted to variety, he is a patchwork fabric, stained by life, marked by the passing instants. Marivaux contrasts the shabby cloth of the poor man with magnificent dress that serves only for gratuitous sparkle: "so many ingots all in vain" (p. 307). Ornate clothing of gold and silver brocade, blindingly ostentatious opulence, "feels neither hunger nor thirst" (p. 307) yet virtually devours man. Unassuming dress is a "mist" (nuée; p. 319) that makes its owner invisible on the great stage of the world. Marivaux's term is well chosen, suggesting at once a mythological nimbus and a nebula of elements. But above all, the tattered rags bring man back to the elements, closer to his void.

[2]

Chardin's Slowness

Already in their own century, Marivaux and Chardin were being compared. A certain Thomas L'Affichard discerned something of the painter's style in Marivaux's comedies: "he writes the way Chardin paints."[1] I wish to explore here another area of common ground connecting these two Regency artists, starting with the dialogue in Chardin's work between labor and leisure, between effort and laziness. Chardin is known as a painter of domestic interiors, a remarkable portraitist of individuals depicted while absorbed in everyday tasks.[2] These paintings led to the nineteenth-century perception of Chardin as a witness to his bourgeois contemporaries and, as Pierre Rosenberg writes, building on a remark made by the Goncourt brothers, to "the hard-working honest bourgeoisie of his time."[3] Charles Blanc writes that Chardin is the historian of "that working class that remains pure in its morals and orderly in its habits."[4] Marcelin Pleynet, who cites these authors in order to illuminate the nineteenth-century appropriation of Chardin—particularly by those who interpret his work as a reflection of his social origins and see him as a working-class artist—underlines this effort to single out Chardin from the other grand masters of the French rococo.

It is important to note, however, that Chardin is equally capable of treating his subjects with a light touch. It is this aspect that I wish to explore here. I turn first of all to his *Bulles de savon* (*Soap Bubbles*; see figure 1), also known as *Le Souffleur de bulles de savon* (*The Soap Bubble Blower*). The subject of this painting is the liquid, airy, vaporous element: Chardin is the perfect painter of the volatile, of sublime evaporation. In the soap bubble he finds the ideal expression of dilation. Introducing into his painting a physics of subtlety, he captures matter in its change of phase: the evolution of the liquid state into the gaseous, the miracle of air, liquid, and vapor; the precarious envelope of vacuous and full. Some critics have associated this painting with the notion of *vanitas*. But the emptiness here is devoid of any theology. René Démoris, with the perspicacity of the psychoanalyst, has written aptly about these "flying bubbles."[5] To him the "bouteilles" or bubbles represent "fleeting wonder," "a fragile object" (*Chardin*, p. 83). The *Encyclopédie* describes the physical delicacy

Figure 1. Jean-Baptiste Siméon Chardin, *Soap Bubbles* (after 1739). Oil on canvas, 60.01 x 73 cm. Gift of the Ahmanson Foundation, Los Angeles County Museum of Art, Los Angeles. Digital image © 2009 Museum Associates/LACMA/Art Resource, NY.

of the bubble, its temporal precarity, thus: "the *bouteille* is quick to burst at the least expansion of the air."[6] This painting also depicts the ephemeral process of ludic creation. The painter, representing himself as lifted up by his "breath," displays his own materiality as light, free-floating, vaporous. The bubble, close to bursting, represents the short-lived, inconsequential piece of work. Like Marivaux, Chardin distances himself from a physics of solids with its borders and concretions. He prefers intermediary states.

This is a universe that defies gravity and weight. A companion painting to the *Bulles,* Chardin's *Les Osselets* (*The Game of Knucklebones*; see figure 2), conjures the same ludic dimension, the same aerial reverie. Both paintings present levitating bodies. Chardin's physics is resolutely unconstrained by the pressure of weight, by any attachment to the ground. His subject is truly "volant" (flying)—indeed, the term figures in the title of another well-known painting by Chardin, the *Fille au volant* (*Girl with a Shuttlecock*). Aerial reverie offers an unfettered alternative to the disciplined absorption that we see in the interior scenes of daily occupations and dutiful activity.

Diderot's remarks (in his *Salon de 1763*) on Chardin's treatment of color resonate within this context. The element of color dilates, evaporates; the plastic mass volatilizes, liquefies, through the painter's technical magic: "Thick layers of color are applied on top of one another and seem to show through the surface from underneath. At other times, it looks as if a mist has been breathed upon the canvas, and elsewhere, a light froth cast upon it."[7] Diderot turns out to be Chardin's ideal reader: he alone grasps the meteorological dimension of this painting, its physics of gases. The chemist is in his element here. He is inspired. If one may speak of the sublime in Chardin, it would have to be understood in terms of this new physics.

The vaporous element is also present in *Dame qui prend son thé* (*A Lady Taking Tea*), in which Chardin combines reverie with the physics of liquids. This painting is haunted by chemistry. Not insignificantly, Chardin's *Un Philosophe occupé de sa lecture* (*A Philosopher Reading*), showing its model in the midst of his vessels and his retort,

Figure 2. Jean-Baptiste Siméon Chardin, *The Game of Knucklebones* (ca. 1734). Oil on canvas, 81.9 x 65.5 cm. The Baltimore Museum of Art: The Mary Frick Jacobs Collection BMA 1938.193.

was initially entitled *Le Souffleur* (*The Blower*). The philosopher is absorbed in studious leisure, in a contemplative bubbling. The vapor combines creative inspiration together with matter.

René Démoris has underlined the peculiarity of Chardin's painting with respect to the representation of action in genre scenes. He shows that Chardin prefers "idle time."[8] He fixes his actors in stillness. Even when painting active subjects, Chardin suspends them in repose. He is precisely the painter of that "instant of *leisure*" ("Nature morte," p. 383). Démoris shows how this technique is extended to the paintings where leisure itself is the subject. Here Chardin chooses passive time, a leisure that in fact leads to "distraction" (p. 384). Démoris neatly defines this moment of "wasted time": "This empty time, which is occupied by nothing . . . is not subject to the time that metes out activity: it gives the feeling of indefinite duration, showing us people simultaneously engaged in an action and detached from it" (p. 384).

Another type of absorption that can be detected in these paintings privileging leisure, recreation, and reverie might lead us to modify the conclusions of the critic Michael Fried. In the *Bulles*, the *Osselets* (that marvelous painting of ephemeral elevation, of aerial suspension), and the *Château de cartes* (*House of Cards*), Fried does observe the element of distraction, but instead of wasted or empty time, he emphasizes the image of *full* time, which makes it possible to signify the autonomy of absorption.[9] But this occupied time would seem more characteristic of absorption in work, as in the domestic scenes. A very different type of absorption is the moralistic kind that can be found in Greuze. There, time is positively *heavy* (with signification, with eroticism). In Greuze's painting *La paresseuse italienne* (*The Lazy Italian Girl*), exhibited in the Salon of 1757, the subject collapses under the weight, the gravity, of her lassitude. Here the painter willingly condones his model's failing, her lack of activity, the fault that weighs her down. The woman is surrounded by unused objects which contemplate her negligence and lack of interest. In contrast, Chardin's sense of distraction is all air and mist: it is a contemplation without consequence.

Chardin's *Château de cartes* (figure 3) belongs to the same register as these idle amusements with their rejection of the universe of work. (A companion piece to this painting is the *Fille au volant*, whose subject, it has been observed, ignores useful objects such as scissors and a pincushion, despite the fact that they are affixed to her clothing.)

In the *Château de cartes*, as well, Chardin conceives a work of fragility. The scaffolding of play is precarious. Similarly, the verse rubrics accompanying Pierre Fillœul's engraving of Chardin's painting highlight inconsistent activity, unstable work. Here too the wind threatens a frivolous construction. Gravitation itself is unsteady:

> Vous vous moquez à tort de cet adolescent
> Et de son inutile ouvrage
> Prest à tomber au premier vent...[10]

> Don't make fun of this boy
> And his futile work
> Ready to topple at the first breeze...

Figure 3. Jean-Baptiste Siméon Chardin, *The House of Cards* (ca. 1736–1737). Oil on canvas, 60.3 x 71.8 cm. Bequeathed by Mrs. Edith Cragg as part of the John Webb Bequest, 1925, National Gallery, London. © National Gallery, London/Art Resource, NY.

Or in Nicolas Bernard Lépicié's text:

> Aimable Enfant que le plaisir décide,
> Nous badinons de nos frêles travaux:
> Mais entre nous, quel est le plus solide
> De nos projets ou bien de vos châteaux.
> (Rosenberg, Chardin, p. 232)

> Delightful Child at pleasure's whim,
> We banter about our fragile works:
> But just between us, which is more solid—
> Our plans or your castles?

What might be called an aesthetics of leisure is perhaps not far removed from Chardin's pictorial practice itself. This painter who claimed to require slowness as a condition of his work ("I take a long time"),[11] and who, as reported by Diderot in his *Salon de 1765,* went so far as to speak of the artist's "torment" and the "difficulty of art,"[12] perfectly represents this transformed time of creation. Démoris mentions Cochin's remark about Chardin's laziness: "In general our friend Chardin was not industrious."[13] We may therefore see his pictorial work as a transcendence, a sublimation of suffering. The effect of laziness is not exactly a rejection of work, but rather its transfiguration into a mastery of time.

Etienne La Font de Saint-Yenne, who was to reproach Chardin for his limited output (Chardin painted slowly and produced little: his corpus amounts to fewer than 300 hundred works, a number that may even be reduced if we consider the artist's tendency to repeat himself; Pierre Rosenberg tallies 200 original subjects) and for indulging in his own "amusement,"[14] attributes to laziness the painter's avoidance of serious painting, the painting of history. For this severe critic, historical painting is uniquely demanding. The historical painter is a dogged worker: he cannot afford leisure and subjects himself to continuous labor. For him free time is an opportunity to devote himself to study:

Moreover the leisure moments of a great Painter of History are rare and precious. After fulfilling what he owes to his religion, his family, his friends, and the society with which he must never dispense, what time can he take for diversion from the great occupations of his profession, if he uses the little time that is left over to work on new paintings?

. . .

> La Peine arrache seule aux Parques leurs ciseaux,
> *Et les avares Dieux vendent tout aux Travaux.*
> (La Font de Saint-Yenne, *Réflexions*, pp. 116–117)

Only labor wrests the scissors from the Fates,
And the miserly Gods sell everything to Work.

What Saint-Yenne finds wanting in Chardin is thus vigilance, toil; this lack relegates him to the status of a minor painter. It may also explain why Chardin's work is somehow shrouded in mystery. Diderot, in his *Salon de 1767*, mentions what might be called the invisibility of this painter's creative effort: "I have never known anyone who actually saw him working."[15] In the same text, Diderot mentions the effect of Chardin's painting on the viewer, the escape from perceptual fatigue offered by the artist's unique magic. Chardin's work is work at rest. The viewer of his paintings experiences a moment of suspension, an idle spell of pleasure. Diderot thinks of it as *recreation*: "the eye is constantly recreated, because there is calm and repose. We stop in front of a Chardin as if by instinct, as a traveler weary from his road will sit, almost unawares, in the spot that offers him a seat of greenery, silence, waters, shade, and cool" (Diderot, *Œuvres esthétiques,* p. 494). Chardin's still lifes must be seen not only as rejecting the glorious representation of actions in clamorous, unruly narrative painting, but as choosing a form of painting that turns inward: the world is confined to rest, in the silence of objects. The hurly-burly of the world is actually inverted into the still life.

Should we see in Chardin's *Les Amusements de la vie privée* (*Domestic Pleasures*) an ironic response, in the form of a self-portrait, to the vexation of the commission? (A matching piece to this painting is *L'Économe* (*The Housekeeper*), whose subject is engrossed in her accounts and seated stiffly at the table for the task at hand.) Here the spinning wheel is still; the closed book suggests the abandonment of reading. La Font de Saint-Yenne sees a "charming lazy woman" in the features of this figure deeply immersed in her idleness, "one arm resting on her lap" (*Réflexions*, p. 136). Subjects in such postures of liquefaction are consistent with an aesthetics of suspended time. One might also detect a vengeful echo, as if in rebuttal to the imaginary self-portrait described as part of the Salon of 1751 in the pages of *Jugements sur les principaux ouvrages exposés au Louvre le 27 août 1751*. Here the spotlight is turned on Chardin, who is represented at the Salon by a very small number of paintings and shown as overcome by laziness:

> The public is vexed never to see more than one painting by such a learned hand. I have been told that he is now working on another one whose singular subject struck me. He is painting himself, with a canvas set in front of him on an easel; a little sprite that represents Nature brings him paintbrushes, which he takes, but at the same time, Fortune takes some of them away, and while he gazes at Laziness who smiles at him indolently, the rest fall from his hands![16]

Playing with Time

Marcelin Pleynet invites us to bypass the moral dilemma that Chardin's painting poses between idleness and work, and to interpret the persistent contradiction as part of the painter's meditation upon time. Referring to *L'Enfant au toton* (*Boy with Top*; see figure 4), Pleynet proposes that we accept the painting as a purely playful

Figure 4. Jean-Baptiste Siméon Chardin, *Boy with Top*.
Oil on canvas, 67 x 76 cm. Musée du Louvre, Paris.
Photo: Erich Lessing/Art Resource, NY.

contemplation, as suspension in play, in the pleasure of playing: this
child happily abandons his books, paper, and pen. Pleynet's observation, with a nod to Heraclitus, that "Time is a child at play" (*Chardin*, p. 68) could serve as the philosophical caption to this painting,
and indeed to the whole of Chardin's work as a time of play.

But Chardin's time also refers to other aspects of his painting,
to his charmed search for those "certain moments" that La Font
de Saint-Yenne identifies negatively as those "utterly uninteresting
actions of life" that are converted into a miracle of "truth" (*Réflexions*, p. 134), or rather of *pleasure*. Chardin, the painter of chemistry,

[47]

enamored of liquid, finds in his totem-top the ideal symbol of the physics implied by his painting. The verses accompanying an engraving of the *Enfant au toton*, while dramatizing the metaphysical dimension, capture the essence of the moment, the random gesture:

Dans les mains du Caprice, auquel il s'abandonne
L'homme est un vrai toton, qui tourne incessamment;
Et souvent son destin dépend d'un mouvement
Qu'en le faisant tourner la fortune lui donne.[17]

In the hands of Caprice, to whom he gives himself,
Man is but a top forever turning;
His fate often depends on one touch
Of fortune as it sets him spinning.

This wondrous infantile object, this small miracle of contradiction that Chardin associates with laziness,[18] is analyzed by Michel Serres in *The Birth of Physics*. The top is at once stable and unstable; it is at rest, yet in motion, spinning and still. The top is literally *circumstance*.[19] In fact, the top resembles the bubble, a miniature world in flux, an ephemeral formation, a contradictory synthetic object: both of them, models of the world, are captured by the painter in a state of wonder. At the same time, Chardin unleashes the ultimate moment of painting: there is movement, but it is paradoxically arrested in representation. He is the perfect painter of circumstance.

The final ironic retort to the accusation of laziness—or, on the other hand, the culmination of a lengthy effort, a life's work reaching completion—occurs when late in life Chardin finally decides to portray himself for the first time, in one of his famous pastels, *Portrait de Chardin aux bésicles* (*Self-Portrait with Spectacles*). Rather than depict himself in ceremonial costume or in his painter's attire, he appears in his nightclothes, with a nightcap knotted on his head. This canvas shows the artist's advanced age alongside the threadbare state of the fabric. No one has described this final still life better than Marcel Proust: "Like the old clothes wrapping his body, his skin too

Figure 5. Jean-Baptiste Siméon Chardin, *Self-portrait, called "abat-jour vert"* (1775). Pastel on gray paper, 46.1 x 38 cm. Musée du Louvre, Paris. Photo: Michèle Bellot/Réunion des Musées Nationaux/Art Resource, NY.

has hardened and worn."[20] If the painter's outfit is, as Proust writes, "fully armed for the night" (p. 18), he seems, in the casual simplicity of his nightclothes, prepared for a final sleep. The painter's apparel is equally modest in another pastel, *Portrait de Chardin à l'abat-jour* (*Portrait of Chardin Wearing an Eyeshade*; see figure 5), where in addition to the kerchief covering his head he wears a visor. He is in front of us, yet seeking the shadows. With his neckscarf and his headwrap, the artist is swathed like a mummy retiring for eternity. He paints himself as if in effigy, at once upright and docile, bound to the inevitability of the void confronting him. Made meek by his failing eyesight, he wields his humble chalk[21] in the final pathetic sign-off of a painter who chose the lesser, the pared-down, the genre of the minimal, the rare.

[3]

The Great Project of an Idle Life

Rousseau

Idleness is one of the contradictory figures that weave through Rousseau's works. He rings all imaginable changes on the notion of inactivity, taking care to tease out the slightest nuances. The problem of idleness pervades Rousseau's philosophical writings and dominates his autobiographical works. My intention here is to trace the various paradoxes that inhabit the question for Rousseau and to explore why it engages him as political philosopher, moralist, and writer alike. After considering his anthropological ruminations on work,[1] as well as his praise of labor, we will see how Rousseau creates a radical esthetics of *désœuvrement* (lack of occupation), the keystone of his program to valorize inactivity and validate subjectivity, which he also envisions as a return to origin. The term *désœuvrement* (desuetude),[2] which Rousseau uses in his *Rêveries du promeneur solitaire* (*The Reveries of the Solitary Walker*) to refer to the inactivity of the body, is well suited to evoke a whole series of meanings not only conveying physical inactivity, but, from a more ontological perspective, referring to the subject himself, de-activated, *without work*, retired from the work.

When Rousseau wrote his *Discours sur les sciences et les arts* (*Discourse on the Sciences and Arts*, 1750), he saw the idler as a non-participant in the public performance of work that defines the citizen. He writes that "every useless citizen may be considered a pernicious man." The idler is among those who "uselessly consume the substance of the State." The crime committed by all these idlers is "misuse of time."[3] In *Emile*, Rousseau develops his formulation of the role of work in validating citizenship. The individual's work becomes the measure of his usefulness and necessity within the community:

> Outside the pale of society, the solitary, owing nothing to any man, may live as he pleases, but in society either he lives at the cost of others, or he owes them in labour the cost of his keep; there is no exception to this rule. Man in society is bound to work; rich or poor, weak or strong, every idler is a thief.[4]

Thus, idleness is decadence, a corruption of natural human energy and an evasion of patriotic duty. Rousseau develops this notion at length in his *Lettre à d'Alembert* (*Letter to d'Alembert*). The banishment of theater from Geneva is intended to prevent idleness from contaminating the social order. The love of theater is seen as nourished by inert passions, by the negative tendencies of boredom. Rousseau is unequivocal: society's collective passion should on the contrary be devoted to work, to constructive activity. Leisure has no place in Rousseau's ideal society: "The good use of time makes time even more precious, and the better one puts it to use, the less one can find to lose. Thus it is constantly seen that the habit of work renders inactivity intolerable and that a good conscience extinguishes the taste for frivolous pleasures."[5] The perfect society is engrossed in activity, in the ritual of work, as illustrated in Rousseau's portrait of the mountain folk living near Neuchâtel—for him the paragon of a small town devoted to useful acts. Idleness, on the other hand, brings evil into the city and promotes unhealthy passions; it is the source of decadence in a community:

> If the country, without commerce, nourishes its inhabitants in inaction, far from fomenting idleness in them, to which they are already only too susceptible because of their simple and easy life, their life must be rendered insufferable in constraining them, by dint of boredom, to employ time usefully which they could not abuse. (*CW* 10: 294)

Presented as the very model of industry, this small town is a shining example of the "prodigies of work" (*Letter to d'Alembert, CW* 10: 294). The work Rousseau praises is in fact an almost "invisible" work, an activity so positive that it might paradoxically be taken for its opposite. The little town pursues an exceptional form of work, magically appearing in the guise of inactivity. The miracle of Neuchâtel's peasant community is that leisure itself is converted into work; every free moment is engaged in some new employment. Putting "spare" time to use is a constant preoccupation. Recreation is the danger that lies in wait for these happy citizens: "I see, in the first place, that their labors will cease to be their amusements and that, as soon as they have a new amusement, it will undermine their taste for the old ones" (*CW* 10: 297). Rousseau's utopian vision seeks to avoid a number of wrongs such as "real time lost" and "slackening of work" (*CW* 10: 297). The only "repose" envisioned is the product of fatigue from labors performed (*CW* 10: 293). It is the ultimate pleasure in store for the exhausted community.

Rousseau ends his *Letter* by asserting the decadence brought about by the theater. In his terms, it is "the meeting place of opulence and idleness" (*CW* 10: 320). Paris, in stark contrast to Geneva, is the quintessential city of idleness, the big city abandoned to *far niente* and depravity. This haven for the vice of inactivity boasts salons and cafés that are full of "do-nothings and rascals" (*CW* 10: 294). Geneva, on the other hand, is the refuge of work, the town that succeeds in presenting work as spectacle:

> The people of Geneva supports itself only by dint of labor and has what is necessary only insofar as it denies itself every excess . . . It seems to me that what ought first to strike every foreigner coming to Geneva is the air of life and activity which prevails there. Everyone is busy, everyone is moving, everyone is about his work and his affairs. I do not believe that any other City so small in the world presents such a spectacle. (*CW* 10: 319)

Rousseau deliberately shows that work even dictates the town's topographical organization, the mode in which it proliferates and expands. Geneva is no less than a paradigm, a tableau of Swiss industry, of European industry in its entirety. Work and population merge in the same space, and through the variety of these industrious activities, the town evinces a hallucinatory effect of overpopulation:

> Visit the St. Gervais Quarter. All the watchmaking of Europe seems centered there. Go through the Molard and the low streets; there, an organization for commerce on a large scale, stacks of boxes, barrels scattered at random, an odor of the Orient and of spices, make you think you are in a seaport. At Paquis and Eaux-Vives the sight and sound of the printed calico and linen mills seems to transport you to Zurich. The city appears, as it were, multiplied by the labors which take place in it; and I have seen people who, at first glance, estimate the population at a hundred thousand souls. (*CW* 10: 319–320)

Fears of unhealthy idleness led Rousseau to propose this hardworking Switzerland as a model for the Corsicans in his *Projet de constitution pour la Corse* (*Plan for a Constitution for Corsica*).[6] He describes the Swiss people as constantly immersed in work, bound to labor by the rigors of the climate and the variety of their pursuits. The Swiss *homo faber* is a *factotum*: "each practiced all the necessary arts in his house; all were masons, carpenters, joiners, wheelwrights" (*CW* 11: 135).

Clearly Switzerland has escaped degeneracy, languishing effeminacy, and decadent indolence. In fact, Geneva belongs to the same class as that other model city so dear to Rousseau: Sparta. For him the paradox of Sparta is the miraculous marriage of work and spectacle—or better yet, the perpetual pedagogy of activity. "It is at Sparta that, in laborious idleness, everything was pleasure and entertainment; it is there that the harshest labors passed for recreations and that small relaxations formed a public instruction" (*Letter to d'Alembert*, *CW* 10: 349). For Rousseau, the only raison d'être of spectacle is its pedagogical effect, as a political strategy within the power structure: an instance of the technology of representation, as understood by Michel Foucault. The spectacle is always a tableau, a representation of society's order and its moral intention.

Rousseau's model community is a group that is broken in by discipline, similar to what Foucault describes in *Discipline and Punish*. In the machine-city or the factory-city, the distribution of forces, the efficient division of labors, and the regularity of work reflect the harmonious coercion of bodies that are effectively rendered docile. This vision of discipline already took a surprising form in the *Discourse on the Sciences and Arts*. Touting the virtues of work, in the same breath Rousseau even lauds "military virtues" and "military exercise" *(Discourse*, 2: 16, 17). And in the *Plan for a Constitution for Corsica*, there is a surprising about-face from the commonplace: it is the laborer who is held up for the soldier's emulation (*CW* 11: 126).

In the *Confessions*, Rousseau returns to the notion of destructive idleness as it occurs in social groups. He cites the salon as an example of unproductivity, of dangerous lack of employment: "I maintain that to make a social circle truly agreeable it is necessary that each not only does something, but something that demands a little attention."[7] In this context, idleness observes a rigid gender distinction, separating men from women. The idleness of women appears as a perversion of nature, its domestication and appropriation by the private space of the salon. When transferred to men, this feminine sedentarity makes monsters of them; the women's quarters become a prison for the men. Rousseau describes these harems of urban idleness: "observe these same men, always constrained in these voluntary prisons, get up, sit down, pace continually back and forth to the fireplace, to the window . . . turn and pirouette about the room, while the idol, stretched out mo-

tionlessly on her couch, has only her eyes and her tongue active"
(*Letter to d'Alembert, CW* 10: 326). Here Rousseau admirably mar-
ries dissipated activity with the idolatry of repose. Socialized indolence, and particularly its worldly exaggeration, constitutes an
inversion of Nature. Nothing can match the fresh air of the Ancients, such as the shepherds: it is the space of virile activity. Exercise and discipline are simply the continuation, the supplement
of Nature herself. It is understandable that the social whirl is often
described as the pure fruit of social idleness, as in this scene from
the *Confessions*:

> Nothing narrows the mind more, nothing engenders more
> trifles . . . than being eternally shut up face to face with an-
> other in a room, reduced to the necessity of continually
> babbling as one's only occupation. . . . What is shocking,
> ridiculous, is in the meantime to see a dozen clods get up,
> sit down, go, come, pirouette on their heels, turn the por-
> celain figures on the mantel around two hundred times,
> and rack their brains to keep up an inexhaustible flow of
> words: a fine occupation! (*CW* 5: 169–170)

For Rousseau, even the "automatons," the well-tuned, docile, silent
machines of the small town, are preferable to these simpering fuss-
budgets, what he calls the "big-city monkeys" (*Letter to d'Alembert,
CW* 10: 294).

In *La Nouvelle Héloïse* (*The New Heloise*), where Rousseau describes the beauty of life in Clarens, we see how artfully idleness
is excluded from this little world. Lack of occupation is carefully
avoided. The landowners' withdrawal itself becomes a continual
effort, a daily repetition of gestures, a sort of invisible activity:

> farm activities replace entertainment. . . . The way they
> spend time here is too simple and too uniform to tempt
> many people; but it is because of the disposition of heart
> of those who have adopted it that it interests them. With

a sound soul, can one tire of discharging the dearest and most charming duties of mankind, and making each other's life happy? Every evening Julie, satisfied with her day, desires nothing different for the morrow, and every morning she asks heaven for a day like the one before: she does always the same things because they are good. . . .[8]

The ingenious secret of the masters of Clarens is to magically transform work into celebration. The description of the grape harvest offers an eloquent tableau of this subtle enterprise: "We sing, we laugh all day long, and the work goes only the better for it" (*The New Heloise, CW* 6: 496). The same formula applies to the servants. Once the daily tasks are done and the burden of work lifted, the temptations of the Sabbath rest, susceptible to corruption in the absence of virtuous labor, are laid open. Recreation is then corralled within the confines of the house under the vigilant eye of the master. The lazy, Saint-Preux observes, are kept under benevolent surveillance.

In Clarens, work is fittingly bucolic. Combining the useful with the pleasant, work is never "hard"; on the contrary, it produces an immediate affective outlet, an aesthetic supplement. Such a mix of work and idleness is dear to the Rousseau who paints the golden age of human society, a dream nourished by Saint-Preux's contemplation of life in Clarens: "One has only to look at the meadows filled with folk tossing hay and singing, and herds scattered in the distance, to be overcome little by little with emotion without knowing why" (*CW* 6: 493).

This rural reverie is extended into the realm of politics in Rousseau's *Plan for a Constitution for Corsica*. He envisions the island under a rustic democratic system in which the laborious life of agriculture prevails and employment fends off all vices: banditry, theft, lust for luxury, and other unhealthy fantasies. The entire island becomes a virtual school for work; everywhere the example of useful activity must be in evidence, at all levels of the social hierarchy.

Rousseau proposes a minutely and justly delineated matrix of land divided into fertile arable territory and barren areas to be reclaimed by industry (factories and forges), and his plan calls for eliminating what he deems the "idle arts" such as sculpture, goldworking, and embroidery (*Corsica*, *CW* 11: 144). In the end, another type of State sovereignty emerges: authority is replaced by activity.

The Origin of Laziness

To consider the question from an anthropological point of view, according to Rousseau's genealogy of societies the state that is closest to idleness is that of the barbarians. His *Essai sur l'origine des langues* (*Essay on the Origin of Languages*) distinguishes three states of human society, corresponding to three original activities: the hunt, as practiced by the savage; herding, the occupation of barbarians; and agriculture, the preserve of civilized man. Rousseau's preference for the isolated situation of the shepherd quickly becomes apparent. In contrast, the hunt, the state of activity par excellence, also manifests the human tendency toward violence and the spirit of conquest, the advent of brute force and war. The agricultural state, associated with the establishment of laws and morality, also entails its share of evils. The pastoral state combines lack of activity with peace, in the virtual absence of industry or property. This is the golden age, the miracle of the first human beings living in isolation, the retreat of the lone shepherd: "The greater number, less active and more peaceable, settled down as soon as they could, gathered livestock, tamed them, made them compliant to the voice of man. . . ; and so began the pastoral life."[9] Here Rousseau echoes Aristotle, who also found the shepherds' life the "laziest": they "lead an idle life, and get their subsistence without trouble from tame animals."[10]

Free of violent encounters, the pastoral life guaranteed personal autonomy: "The pastoral art, father of repose and of the idle passions, is the one that is most self-sufficient" (*Essay*, *CW* 7: 309). Rousseau indulges his dream of the sweet primordial days when men were spared the duties and necessity of association with others. Here is the paradise of indolence:

> Assume a perpetual spring on earth; assume water, livestock, pasturage everywhere; assume men leaving the hands of nature, once dispersed throughout all this: I cannot imagine how they would ever have renounced their primitive freedom and forsaken the isolated and pastoral life so suited to their natural indolence, in order needlessly to impose on themselves the slavery, the labors, the miseries inseparable from the social state. (*Essay*, *CW* 7: 310)

Rousseau adds to this passage a crucial note in which he paints original man, natural man, as lazy. Activity is simply not natural to man. It is actually a perversion of man's inclinations, and leads to catastrophic consequences. Activity is, essentially, the fruit of social adaptation, but it is conditioned by laziness. The subject comes full circle when he rediscovers his original repose:

> The extent to which man is naturally lazy is inconceivable. One would say that he lives only in order to sleep, to vegetate, to remain immobile; he can scarcely resolve to devote the motions necessary to prevent himself from dying of hunger. Nothing upholds the love of so many savages for their state as this delightful indolence. The passions that make a man restless, provident, active, are born only in society. To do nothing is man's first and strongest passion after that of self-preservation. Were this considered carefully, it would be seen that even among us it is in order to achieve repose that each works; it is still laziness that makes us industrious. (*CW* 7: 310 note)

The very same anthropological hypothesis, positing the primacy of laziness, can be found in the *Dialogues* (*Rousseau, Judge of Jean-Jacques*). The human experience, at its origins, was one of leisure and relaxation: "All men are naturally lazy, even their interest doesn't animate them. . . . But as amour-propre is progressively aroused, it excites them, pushes them. . . . The man who is not dominated by amour-propre and who does not go seeking his happiness far from himself is the only one who knows heedlessness and sweet leisure."[11] The return to solitary idleness that Rousseau defends elsewhere is thus explained by the fact that in the beginning, in nature, idleness is dissociative. The "great project of that idle life" announced in the *Confessions* (*CW* 5: 536) thus seeks a positive regression of the subject, a redemptive reversal. The subject simply regains the originary passion for "doing nothing." This new condition might take its motto from the *Letter to d'Alembert*, written in the defensive phase of Rousseau's work: *vitam impendere otio*, to devote one's life to leisure.

Full-Length Portrait of the Idler

Rousseau's endorsement of idleness in his autobiographical texts can be understood in this light. He willingly confides his penchant for laziness, his innate indolence. At least, that is one side of his conflicted persona, which moves from agitation to paralyzing lassitude. In Rousseau's *Lettres à Malesherbes*, we find this revealing self-portrait: "A lazy soul that gets frightened at every effort, a temperament that is ardent, bilious, easily affected and excessively sensitive to everything that affects it do not seem capable of being joined together, nevertheless these two opposites make up the basis of mine."[12] The *Dialogues* underline the same contradiction within Jean-Jacques himself: "He is active, ardent, laborious, indefatigable; he is indolent, lazy, without vigor" (*Dialogues*, *CW* 1: 122).[13]

But idleness takes on a positive value for Rousseau only when it is reclaimed by solitude.[14] Here again, the *Dialogues* are instructive:

"For indolence and idleness, which are such a great vice in society, are so no longer in anyone who has renounced the advantages of society not to endure its work" (*CW* 1: 127). This is why Diderot's condemnation of solitary retreat as "inhuman" would cut Rousseau to the quick. Rousseau corrected Diderot's assertion—"Only the wicked person is alone"[15]—with his own decisive inversion: "Whoever suffices to himself does not want to harm anyone at all" (*Dialogues, CW* 1: 100). The solitary individual shuns activity as well as toil and "intrigues in the world" (*Dialogues, CW* 1: 127). Solitary idleness thus converges with the classical ideal of the *vita contemplativa*, escaping the ills of society. Walter Benjamin recognizes this condition of solitude as Rousseau's means of access to "authentic idleness,"[16] the "eternal leisure" described in the *Confessions* (*CW* 5: 536).

The *Dialogues* consistently describe a "[c]ontemplative J.J." (*CW* 1: 121). Rousseau's laziness becomes above all a *mental* laziness. It requires the suspension of all intellectual activity, the cessation of any mental fatigue.[17] Rousseau dated to the period of the first *Discourse* his original exit from the world of liberty and his fateful entry into celebrity. Suddenly the subject is weighed down, as recalled in *The Reveries of a Solitary Walker*: "thrown into a literary career by foreign impulsions, I felt the fatigue of mental work" (*Reveries, CW* 8: 58). Contemplation must therefore take place when the head is at rest. Sketching his self-portrait in the *Confessions*, Rousseau describes his "slowness in thinking": "I have to wait," he recalls simply (*Confessions, CW* 5: 95). The *Dialogues* also depict J.J.'s distraction, the ideal state of "laziness about thinking" (*Dialogues, CW* 1: 115). This is a particular form of distraction, in which the subject is precisely "thinking of nothing" (*Dialogues, CW* 1: 115; translation modified). But in the same text, Rousseau explains the above-mentioned paradox of Jean-Jacques: "He cannot tolerate absolute idleness. His hands, his feet, his fingers must move, his body must be exercised, and his head must remain at rest. That is the source of his passion for walking, which allows him to move without being obliged to think. In reverie, one is not active" (*Dialogues*, *CW* 1: 143). The point is emphasized: "The contemplative life discourages action" (*Dialogues*, *CW* 1: 125). The tension between agitation and lethargy that splits Rousseau's very being is what determines the writer's participation in all forms of idleness.

We may deduce that Rousseau seeks to avoid the perception of a glorious, ostentatious idleness like the classical *otium* with its cachet, its supplement of dignity. The important distinction he makes can be summed up by the phrase *faire plus; ne faire nulle chose*, from the description of the utopian isle of Papimania that he cites in the *Confessions*: "Where one does more, where one does nothing" (*CW* 5: 536). This is a turbulent idleness, paradoxically founded on continuous movement:

> The idleness I love is not that of a do-nothing who stays there with his arms crossed in total inactivity and thinks no more than he acts. It is both that of a child who is cease-lessly in motion while doing nothing and, at the same time, that of a dotard who strays when his arms are at rest. I love to occupy myself by doing trifles, beginning a hun-dred things and finishing none of them, going and coming as the fancy comes into my head, changing plans at each instant, following a fly in all its flying about, wanting to uproot a rock to see what is under it, undertaking a labor of ten years with ardor, and abandoning it without regret after ten minutes, in sum, musing all day long without or-der and without sequence, and following only the caprice of the moment in everything. (*Confessions*, *CW* 5: 537)

Laziness is what orders Rousseau's entire moral persona. He seeks to withdraw from the universe of action. Jean-Jacques is car-ried away by a "laziness of the will" (*Dialogues*, *CW* 1: 144) which removes him from the world of reflection, of amour-propre—in short, from society. This is what impels him to throw himself into a series of pursuits that could be described as invisible: for example, copying music, which Rousseau tells us is suited to his "lazy mind" (*Dialogues*, *CW* 1: 138). He adjusts easily to his middling financial condition: neither ease nor penury. His intellectual work is measured by the same yardstick of moderation. He must avoid the fatigue of work, especially when it is linked with the obligation to produce books. Thought must be free, disengaged from necessity: "If I sometimes like to think, it is freely and without constraint, letting my ideas flow at will without subjecting them to anything. But thinking of this or of that as an obligation, as a trade, making my productions correct, methodical is for me the work of a galley slave" (*Dialogues*, *CW* 1: 139). Rousseau thus sets his output apart by withholding it from the market, applying the label "livrier" ("book factory"; *Dialogues*, *OC* 1: 840; *CW* 1: 139) to the writer who produces books for money or the author who is incapable of the "disinterestedness" essential to the "products of [the] soul" (*Dialogues*, *CW* 1: 139). The "book factory" also recalls Rousseau's description of those toiling in the realm of scientific activity: both suffer from "the itch to talk" (*Dialogues*, *CW* 1: 139).

Laziness as a withdrawal from the world of will places Rousseau within a cluster of marginal figures whose stance of philosophical indigence is an acceptance of circumstances, a refusal to accumulate material wealth, a form of economic resistance. Laziness becomes sluggishness of desire, an apathy with regard to objects. Rousseau describes this attitude of Jean-Jacques's: "Another prop for his laziness in any affair that was a little lengthy was the uncertainty time places on successes which seem the most assured in the future, a thousand unforeseen events being capable of aborting the best conceived plans at any moment" (*Dialogues*, *CW* 1: 152). Laziness is a friend of circumstance. It falls in step with probabilities. Jean-Jacques chooses to "live from day to day" (*Dialogues*, *CW* 1: 143).[18]

In his autobiographical works, Rousseau proposes a series of activities that constitute a veritable scandal of nonproduction.

Indeed, he admires the spectacle of inactivity. A case in point is the musical score at which he plugs away endlessly, accumulating errors and deletions, making deliberately slow progress on the project. Laziness naturalizes his work, for slowness is nature's true speed: "He works slowly and ponderously, makes many mistakes, erases or starts over ceaselessly" (*Dialogues, CW* 1: 145). His laziness even accommodates toil and persistent effort. Then there are the laces he makes. In the *Confessions,* he recounts how this activity allowed him to stave off boredom "in the most perfect inaction" (*Confessions, CW* 5: 503). Lacemaking is the very model of his project of inactivity: "I went to work at my door like the women and chatted with passersby" (*Confessions, CW* 5: 503). Rousseau is conscious of the strangeness to which his lacemaking consigns him. In his *vita otiosa,* "a tranquil and sweet life" (*Confessions, CW* 5: 503), he also adopts feminine habits: "I make laces: I am more than half woman" (*Confessions, OC* 1: 1572, note 3). Through all these pursuits, these pseudo-activities, Rousseau experiences the "simplicity of true Genius" among Neuchâtel's contented artists as extolled in his *Letter to d'Alembert* (*CW* 10: 294). Work as amusement implies routine, mechanical repetition, the complete suspension of effort.

Of course, the most radical forms of inactivity for Rousseau remain the reverie and the promenade. Both of these complement the contradiction of Rousseau's idleness. Reverie, the quintessential form of mental laziness, the intellectual suspension of will, makes it possible to ignore the body in favor of the imagination. It is the gateway to the contemplative life. Reverie is the disgusted opposite of action, in a sense its anti-matter. The *Dialogues* clarify the nature of reverie as a unique form of passivity of the subject, a singular dispossession of the will. Rousseau says that "one enjoys without acting" (*CW* 1: 143).[19] As for the promenade, it incorporates the restless side of laziness, but still produces nothing. The promenade does not engage the will. It merely accompanies the subject, tracing the path of its freedom: "He will always repeat the same [walk] until some motive absolutely forces him to change.

His feet carry him back by themselves to where they have already carried him. He likes to walk straight ahead always, because that can be done without his needing to think about it" (*Dialogues*, *CW* I: 144).[20] The text that sums up to perfection this double figure of idleness is *The Reveries of the Solitary Walker*.

The Laziness of Being

Rousseau's *Reveries*, written late in life (1772–1778), illuminate his deliberate intention to bring forth another body, one that is liberated from all constraints, that escapes all relations of knowledge and power. In fact, the *Reveries* reproduce, in an inverted form, the entire technology of surveillance over the subject. Rousseau's autobiographical project in this text must be plainly understood as an enterprise of untethered individualization, apolitical in the sense of being detached from the various sites of power and from all forms of relation. This is what Rousseau calls his "désœuvrement" ("desuetude"): an attempt to disengage his body, to air out its materiality, to objectively *nullify* his person (*Rêveries*, *OC* I: 1000; *CW* 8: 7).

Rousseau proposes the *Reveries* as an "examination" (*CW* 8: 7). But here the gesture of observation is strictly interior. It takes the form of a self-surveillance that is disoriented, utterly without constraint, a meditation that dispenses with any results and dreads any science of the self. This examination is a volatile, fruitless operation. From the start, Rousseau eliminates order and method:

> I am incapable of such work, and it would even take me away from my goal, which is to make myself aware of the modifications of my soul and of their sequence. I will perform on myself, to a certain extent, the measurements natural scientists perform on the air in order to know its daily condition. I will apply the barometer to my soul, and these

measurements, carefully executed and repeated over a long period of time, may furnish me results as certain as theirs. But I do not extend my enterprise that far. I will be content to keep a record of the measurements without seeking to reduce them to a system. (*CW* 8: 7–8)

The *Reveries* must be seen as a follow-up, supplement, or appendix to the *Confessions*, but from a position that takes a less burdensome approach to self-revelatory protocol. Here Rousseau seeks to distance himself from any legalistic defense. The *Confessions* promised a "severe . . . examination" (*CW* 5: 6); this was also the case with their juridico-schizophrenic extension in the *Dialogues*. The return to himself in the *Reveries*, by contrast, aims at lightness and buoyancy. Hence the text's materiality as "feuilles" (leaves) which constitute a "shapeless," improvised journal (*Reveries, OC* 1: 1000; *CW* 8: 7). The *Reveries* intend to be pure pleasure, unburdened by the moral weight of avowals, or by the contortions of guilt. The examination of the subject that is undertaken here pursues only the ephemeral, the everyday.[21] It chooses to forget the past. The *Reveries* are written in the lightness of inconsistency. The First Promenade, proposing the barometer as an instrument appropriate to the journal, points to a physics of aeration, a chemistry of the volatile, in short the meteorology of the soul that governs Rousseau's entire enterprise.

Undoubtedly the Fifth Promenade provides the best illustration of this new phase for Jean-Jacques. This is where he most clearly illustrates the uselessness of the subject. What has been seen as the outline of an autonomous subject can be understood here through the complexly constructed asceticism of the individual freed from the constraints of time. Abandoning calculated time, Rousseau's promenade is devoted to the unrestricted schedule, the irregularity of whimsy, the individual's idiosyncrasy. He seeks a state in which "time is nothing. . . ; in which the present lasts forever without, however, making its duration noticed and without any trace of time's passage" (*CW* 8: 46). Rousseau reports his happiness during a delightful retreat to the Ile de Saint-Pierre: "The precious *far niente* was the first and the principal enjoyment I wanted to savor in all its sweetness, and all I did during my sojourn was in effect only the delightful and necessary pursuit of a man who has devoted himself to idleness" (*CW* 8: 42).

This moment in the *Reveries* which re-imagines a new concept of time can be juxtaposed to a key episode in the *Dialogues*, a fundamental step in the so-called reform project, in which Rousseau relates how Jean-Jacques emancipates himself from his watch: "The moment when he got rid of his watch, renouncing all thought of becoming rich in order to live from day to day, was one of the sweetest days of his life. Heaven be praised, he cried in a fit of joy, I won't need to know what time it is any longer" (*Dialogues*, *CW* 1: 143). Jean-Jacques delivers himself from the disciplinary clock to enter into a personal, internalized time, without rule or constraint—an idiosyncratic time of which he is the sole master, in which he loses track of time. He bids good riddance to mechanical, regimented, profitable time, to any sort of *timetable*. Detaching himself from the Genevan instrument of measurement par excellence—also a symbol of growing industrialization—is perhaps the most anti-Protestant (or anti-Calvinist) gesture in Rousseau's body of work.[22] Instead, the time that Rousseau inhabits in the solitariness of those emblematic occupations mentioned earlier—copying music, lacemaking, and writing—is time that would escape economic exploitation, that avoids uniformity, linearity, the exactitude of succession.

Thus repose, the foundation of pleasure, is opposed to work and to production. The cultivation of the self depends on pure idleness, on being oblivious to utilitarian action. *To do nothing*, literally, is to shun the world's materiality in favor of investment in one's inner self: "Movement which does not come from outside then occurs inside us" (*Reveries*, *CW* 8: 47). Rousseau also endeavors to free the soul from the body's carceral shell. Michel

Foucault's characterization of the soul in the eighteenth century as "the prison of the body,"[23] the internalized seat of constraints imposed on the body, is well known. Jean-Jacques's pursuit of liberation thus takes on not only the subjugated organ but also its ideal existential effect. Idleness as the effacement of the exterior makes it possible to nourish the interior life of pure psychic activity. And the latter is itself subjected to a minimum of constraints: reasoning is abandoned; pure unmediated affection, or affective reminiscence, prevails. In the end, even the activity of writing is doomed to inactivity. The notation of the reverie or promenade, in its avoidance of any stricture, obeys the order of *far niente*, of absolute amusement, that is, of occupation as a *waste* of time. It then becomes apparent that the *Reveries* are from the outset condemned to incompletion.

Later, Rousseau proposes botany as the solitary walker's exemplary activity: "Botany is a study for an idle and lazy solitary person." He adds: "In this idle occupation there is a charm we feel only in the complete calm of the passions" (*Reveries, CW* 8: 64). Just what is it about botany? If this activity enjoys Rousseau's approval, it is because he conceives it as fundamentally disinterested, requiring barely any investment of the body; it harmonizes with the "luxurious idleness" desired by the subject (*CW* 8: 47). If botany is still a form of work, it is not "toilsome work" but rather "amusing [work]"; (*CW* 8: 43). The promenade, the same activity that Rousseau considers as the botanist's "sole task,"[24] is also a form of recreation in which the freely wandering gaze observes without regard to profit or instruction. Jean-Jacques eliminated other activities because they could impose constraints, yoking the organism extensively to activity. He thus bars himself from forms of knowledge applied to industry. In the *Reveries*, botany enjoys the advantage of existing apart from a utilitarian hierarchy of techniques. Rousseau reaches his decision through negative deduction. Thus, he rejects mineralogy for its deleterious demands:

To make progress in the study of minerals, it is necessary to be a chemist and a physicist. It is necessary to perform tedious and costly experiments, to work in laboratories, to spend much money and time in the midst of charcoal, crucibles, furnaces, retorts, smoke, and suffocating fumes, always at the risk of life and often at the expense of health. (*CW* 8: 63)

The study of the animal kingdom also elicits reproaches: "How am I to observe, dissect, study, become acquainted with the birds in the air, the fish in the water, or the quadrupeds swifter than the wind and stronger than man, which are no more disposed to come offer themselves to my research than I to run after them to make them submit to it by force?" (*CW* 8: 63). In contrast to these two pursuits, botany imposes nothing on the body; it compels no form of instrumentality. The botanist's tools require no codification of the body: "a point and a magnifying glass are all the apparatus he needs" (*CW* 8: 64). They are a non-binding extension of the organs that they supplement: in this case, the eye and the hand. In Rousseau's vision, botany taps into a simple, virtually infantile sensationism, which mobilizes only the primary organs, the primary instruments of the senses: the hand and the eye.[25] Here we also see a detachment from any form of work involving the intervention of tools.

Perhaps in Rousseau's eyes the most abject image of the laborer is that of the metalsmith, who engages in artificial and excessive forms of industry, in the obsessive, covert, nocturnal pursuit of natural riches. Even further opposed to the metalworker than the botanist is the shepherd, who in a sense embodies the worker in a state of redemption. Rousseau pictures pastoral work as bathed in the glow of sunlight, in the grace of nature and its contemplation. In fact, he even suggests, the shepherd *does not work*: he is the immediate recipient of the natural objects that are placed "within his reach." The shepherds and "robust plowmen" of the *Reveries* are free to indulge in amorous pastimes (*CW* 8: 62–63).

The writer's study thus becomes a locus of dystopia in Rousseau's work. Jean-Jacques makes every effort to transform the confined space of the cabinet into its opposite. Only when transplanted into nature can he produce work: "I never do anything except while taking a walk, the countryside is my study; the sight of a table, some paper, and books bores me."[26] The *Dialogues* propose an opposition between botany and pharmacy. Rousseau describes a laboratory, with its stills, ovens, heads, and converters (*Dialogues*, *CW* 1: 135); in contrast, his favored work space is "out in the fields" (*CW* 1: 134). If the pharmaceutical enterprise is reduced to the display of "cartons filled with the stalks of plants . . . and seeds sorted into little, classified boxes" (*CW* 1: 134), by contrast Rousseau's botanical pursuits entail no assault upon the interiority or integrity of his objects of study, no chemical transformation such as pulverization or distillation. They are summoned only through visual contact, through the botanist's naked eye.

The herbarium that forms such a deliberate part of the botanist's activity stands out as a form of non-work, a non-scientific activity. Rousseau is careful to distinguish it from the academic approach to botany. His *herbier* is not (as defined in the *Encyclopédie*) "a treatise on plants";[27] it disregards rigorous classification; it is not a "botany textbook."[28] The objects encountered on a walk are immediately, spontaneously selected for preservation: "with each new blade of grass I encounter, I say to myself with satisfaction: here is yet another plant" (*Reveries*, *CW* 8: 58). The plants and flowers assembled by the collector are not signs. They could be considered hieroglyphs. Belonging to an affective, ornamental semiotics, they are more souvenir than written record. As the traces of pure observation, they give themselves up only to observation. Rousseau's herbaria are, as he terms them, "mémoratifs" (reminders);[29] they represent a stasis, a slow suspension in the stages of the promenade, a poetic pause, a way to freeze the fleeting. They bear witness to an encounter, a captured circumstance. There is no real method in these herbaria: only the collection, the serendipitous gathering of odd moments. Botany traces a topography of the random, a nomadic pursuit of forgetfulness:

> To wander nonchalantly in the woods and in the country, here and there to take up mechanically, sometimes a flower, sometimes a branch; to graze on my fodder almost at random, to observe the same thing thousands of times, and always with the same interest because I always forgot them, was enough for me to pass eternity without being bored for a moment. (*Confessions, CW* 5: 537)

Moreover, the promenade can easily end without any collection taking place, leaving the walker with only the memory of the plants: "My manner of herborizing is to wander randomly in the countryside, and to observe right and left the plants which strike me, often without even uprooting them in order to dissect them."[30] And if at first the botanical project seems to re-introduce scientific ambitions of systematization and taxonomy (as, for example, on the island of Saint-Pierre: Rousseau planned his *Flora petrinsularis* on the model of Linnaeus's *Systema naturae*), it becomes evident that this project is reduced to a poetics of the insignificant and inconsequential, in which the total picture is overshadowed by eccentric details: meadow hay, lichen, wood moss, blade of grass, plant particle . . . In the same Fifth Promenade, scientific differentiation produces a magical litany of plant names: *Brunelle, Balsamine, Buis, Ortie* (Self-heal, Touch-me-not, Boxwood, Nettle; *Rêveries, OC* 1: 1043; *CW* 8: 43).

We may now turn to one of the most surprising moments in the *Rêveries*, in the Seventh Promenade: the solitary plant-collecting excursion that brings Rousseau to the doors of a stocking mill. Of course this episode can be read as the unconscious reactivation of Rousseau's paranoia as he re-encounters within his idyllic spot of isolation and refuge the human contacts he had fled, his "persecutors" (*Reveries, CW* 8: 65). Rousseau's botanical reverie is interrupted by a certain repetitive "clanking" that "was repeated and increased" (*CW* 8: 66): the rhythmic noise of the factory, the cadence of work, the rhythm of the machine itself. Here extreme singularity comes face to face with the anonymous mechanical apparatus of "human industry": "I got up, burst through a thicket of brush on the side from which the noise was coming, and, in a little hollow twenty feet from the very place where I believed myself to have been the first to arrive, I saw a stocking mill" (*CW* 8: 66). How vexing for the lazy botanist to stumble upon this factory buzzing with workers![31]

Rousseau is repelled by such agitation, which flies in the face of the true philosophical attitude of exquisite repose. Hannah Arendt's distinction between labor and work, put forth in *The Human Condition*, may shed light on this passage of the *Reveries*. Arendt emphasizes the new rhythm brought to bear by the industrial machine. The machine is thus distinguished from the tools of *homo faber*: work, which used to involve individual, separate gestures, becomes labor as the machine imposes a collective "rhythmically ordered performance." Arendt develops this notion beautifully: "it is . . . the machine's movement which enforces the movements of the body. The point is that nothing can be mechanized more easily and less artificially than the rhythm of the labor process." In the final analysis, the alienation of *homo faber* from his tools and the substitution of the machine result in the disappearance of the human body's own natural rhythm.[32]

In the *Confessions*, when Rousseau becomes aware of his physical decline, his "machine in decay" (*CW* 5: 207), the activities he contemplates are on the cusp of work and idleness. At Charmettes, as he imagines his approaching death, rustic activities become the occupation of his involuntary retirement. He describes the harvesting of grapes and other fruits. At the same time, however, as his frailty worsens, he is progressively reduced to the role of idle spectator: "when I had given six blows with a spade, I was out of breath, sweat streamed down me, I could not do any more" (*CW* 5: 195–196). Later, Rousseau witnesses the prowess of Wintzenried, his new rival in Madame de Warens's household. Seeing Wintzenried in action—the man is is not shy about flaunting his vigorous physique—is the last straw for Rousseau. The newcomer to Charmettes is a hyperactive Hercules: "His great pleasure was to pick up and carry, to saw or split wood, one always saw him with an axe or pick in his hand; one heard him running, thumping, shouting at the top of his lungs. I do not know how many men's work he did" (*CW* 5: 219–220). Madame de Warens's woodsplitter sends Rousseau back to the study and contemplation that fill him with ambivalence. The strongman's ax and pick contrast with Rousseau's books of dreamy, unproductive musings, the distractions of learning.

An Ethics of Liberty

In *The Reveries of the Solitary Walker*, Rousseau presents for our contemplation an ascetic construction of the self that sheds the template of constraint. What must be heard in the project of retreat that he envisions in his final days is the insistent call of liberty. If this is a text written against the Enlightenment and its philosophes, we must read Rousseau's criticism as upholding the languid triumph of liberty: "I could not bear subjection; I was perfectly free and better than free, for bound only by my affections, I did only what I wanted to do" (*Reveries, CW* 8: 90). The subject shuns every obligation, renounces all activity; he avoids *doing* on principle: "I abstain from acting, for all of my weakness is with regard to action, all of my strength is negative," and opposes himself to others who are compulsively "busy, restless" (*CW* 8: 56). He finds a paradoxical, critical reconciliation between inaction and will, proffered as the foundation of a new conduct, an ontological attitude, an ethics of freedom: "I no longer have any other rule of conduct than in everything to follow my own propensity without restraint" (*CW* 8: 57). Once again Jean-Jacques becomes the "free agent" par excellence of the second *Discourse*, the performer of "purely spiritual acts," those gestures that define his humanity and remove him from the mechanical universe.[33] More precisely, the "scandal" of Rousseau's conception of freedom (indeed, this is where he perceives the radical nature of his approach) must be understood according to a doubly negated injunction adopted by the subject: *"never doing what he does not want to do"* (*CW* 8: 56). Gilles Deleuze would see this formulation of Rousseauist freedom as fitting squarely within the "logic of negative preference."[34] The grammar of Rousseau's phrase indeed emphasizes the solitary subject's singular condition, which imposes its reactive but absolute selectivity with respect to all forms of action.

Rousseau makes laziness the very motor of the lack of will, of the abandonment of will.[35] This inertia is governed above all by the relation to the self, as he explains in the *Dialogues*: "Rebellious to any other will, he doesn't even know how to obey his own, or rather he finds it so tiring even to will that he prefers in the course of living to follow a purely mechanical impression that carries him along without his having to direct it" (*Dialogues*, *CW* 1: 144). Moreover, laziness of will becomes Rousseau's explanatory term for all other negations of activity. It must be aligned with "laziness about thinking" (*Dialogues*, *CW* 1: 115) and "reluctance to talk" (*CW* 1: 110). In this supreme inertia of will there is a form resembling what Giorgio Agamben analyzes in connection with Heidegger's "originary possibilitization" (*"die ursprüngliche Ermöglichung"*).[36] This aspect of laziness shares the same experience of "being-held-in-suspense." Agamben describes the manifestation of this "originary possibilitization" as follows: it "constitutively has the form of a potential-not-to [*potenza-di-no*], of an impotentiality, insofar as it is *able to* [*può*] only in beginning from a *being able not to* [*poter non*], that is, from a deactivation of single, specific, factical possibilities" (p. 67).

However, it is clear that Rousseau's *vita otiosa* achieves transfiguration only at a cost—by renouncing history, renouncing life itself in an impatient quest for disappearance. The desire for an infinite suspension of time brings time to a standstill. The realization of the subject, its epiphany, coincides with death, the ultimate retreat. In the end, the laziness of being coincides with the subject's final blackout. To invoke the historical "inversion" of the rankings of *vita contemplativa* and *vita activa*, well-known from Hannah Arendt's characterization of modernity, the purity of Rousseau's quest for uselessness can be seen as a sort of reform. His articulation of a "work" of laziness and his detachment from the corporeal constraints of the universe of work converge toward that particular asceticism of the subject which is the serene and radical murmur of liberty. The meaning of the word *paresse* captures all the conceptual hesitations of his discourse: it goes from idleness to indolence, from lapse to leisure, from negligence to rest. In the end, we prefer the catchword *désœuvrement*, comprising work itself in suspension, in the process of undoing, like the subject itself in dissolution.

[4]

Paradox of the Idler

Diderot

Like Marivaux, Diderot makes the idler into a figure of modernity—but he adds an intriguing twist. Like his close ancestor, the Indigent Philosopher, Diderot's idler appears in urban space. In the title character of *Le Neveu de Rameau* (*Rameau's Nephew*, 1762–1777), the author offers an example of alternative subjectivation. The dialogue between the philosopher and the vagabond brings face to face two opposing figures of idleness—and two opposing relationships to the work. On the one hand there is the philosopher, addicted to his philosophical promenade, his meditative strolls: "Come rain or shine, my custom is to go for a stroll in the Palais-Royal every afternoon at about five. I am always to be seen there alone, sitting on a seat in the Allée d'Argenson, meditating."[1] But thought quickly yields to circumstance, escaping all constraints. Like Marivaux's Spectator, Diderot's philosopher enjoys free-floating, vaporous thought. Placing himself straightaway at the center of a ferment of ideas, a fertile multiplicity, he is eager to leave behind the solitary leisure of his ordinary introspection, his temporary self-centeredness:

> I hold discussions with myself on politics, love, taste or philosophy, and let my thoughts wander in complete abandon, leaving them free to follow the first wise or foolish idea that comes along, like those young rakes we see in the Allée de Foy who run after a giddy-looking little piece with a laughing face, sparkling eye and tip-tilted pose, only to

leave for another, accosting them all, but sticking to none. In my case my thoughts are my wenches. (*Nephew*, p. 33)

The philosopher is already following his penchant for freedom, for unconstrained thought and joyful dissipation. Diderot's philosopher is meteorological, adapting to the weather of the moment; he knows the art of whiling away the time: "If it is too cold or wet I take shelter in the Café de la Régence and amuse myself watching people play chess" (p. 33). This is where habit meets happenstance, producing an encounter like no other: his meeting with the exceptional Rameau. Moreover, the surroundings in which Diderot places these two characters is a site associated with *far niente*, a regular den of vagrant idlers. Louis-Charles Fougeret de Monbron seizes upon the coffeehouse as a haven for idleness, for wasted time: "idleness brings so many shirkers together there."[2] Rousseau would hardly disagree, consigning to the same lot "the coffee houses and the houses of ill fame."[3] Rameau himself is surprised to find the philosopher there: "what are you doing here among all this lot of idlers?" (p. 36). How can we explain the fascination this character held for Diderot, who in contrast not only labored tirelessly on his own great work, the *Encyclopédie*, but also personally saw to completion the work of numerous contributors (five thousand entries, as calculated by experts), especially when these "lazy" writers quit or dragged their feet?[4]

In short, Diderot confronts the restless philosopher with this vagabond, a hero of indiscipline. Rameau himself exclaims: "You know of course that I am an ignoramus, a fool, a lunatic, rude, lazy" (p. 45). Elsewhere he goes so far as to call himself an "idler" (p. 123), a "*fainéant*."[5] In his *Dictionnaire des synonymes* Condillac, grouping idleness, laziness, and *fainéantise* together under the rubric "désœuvrement" (inactivity) establishes distinctions based on differences of social status and economic condition, which shed an interesting light on Diderot's dialogue. Idleness, for example, presupposes ease; laziness is selective inactivity. As for *fainéan-*

tise, it is a consequence of poverty. Condillac's condemnnation of this state is unconditional, so unnatural does the rejection of the world of work appear to him: "*Fainéantise*, from *faire néant* [to do nothing], is the condition of a wretch who doesn't even want to work to procure the essentials of life. The term is applied only to vagabonds, beggars, and those in need because they absolutely refuse to do anything."[6] Condillac's distinctions cannot defeat the persistence of a certain idleness conceived as positive—the aristocratic variety, the indolence of a class unfamiliar with laborious activity, free from necessity. *Fainéantise* is relegated, along with laziness, to the bottom of the ladder of inactivity. Both consist in the refusal to work by those who are supposed to, constrained as they are by the necessity of *doing*.

Diderot clearly places Rameau at the lowest point in this chain of idlers, the better to radicalize his character's situation. The Nephew devotes himself to absolute idleness, an insolent extreme of *far niente*. In the course of the dialogue he numbers laziness among his faults, applying to himself the epithets used by his sponsors: "Rameau the lunatic, impertinent, ignorant, lazy, greedy old fool" (p. 46). He confirms his "role as an idler, fool and good-for-nothing" (p. 68). His goal is essentially to avoid any situation of subjugation. Despite his parasitic status, he paradoxically claims: "I am quite prepared to be abject, but not under compulsion" (p. 70).

Diderot's buffoon shuns the universe of work. He studiously avoids all sites of production or, more precisely, he operates in their margins. Diderot makes him a congenial parasite: "But I must have a good bed, good food, warm clothes in the winter and cool ones in summer, leisure, money and lots of other things, and I would rather owe them to charity than have to work for them" (p. 123). The Nephew's parasitism consists of derailing the production machine, of using ruses to liquidate the capital of others, whatever its origin. This parasitism makes sense in a general economy that the Nephew characterizes as a system of restitution, a chain of vengeance that mirrors the natural food chain: "We mete out justice to each other without the law taking a hand. The Deschamps female formerly, and more recently the Guimard, are the King's vengeance upon the financier, and now dressmaker, jeweller, furnisher, laundry-woman, swindler, chamber-maid, cook, harness-maker are avenging the financier upon the Deschamps" (p. 63). Only Rimbaud, a century later, can really hold a candle to Rameau. He belongs to the race of magnificent reprobates, among whom he lays particular claim to a legacy of lying and laziness. Rimbaud proclaims his hatred of the nineteenth century as a "siècle à mains" ("century of hands"). "I am horrified by all occupations," he declares in his "Mauvais sang": "lazier than a toad," he cherishes his idleness.[7] Rameau could also adopt the words of an anonymous contemporary whose pamphlet, the *Éloge de la paresse, dédié à un moine* (1778), justifies the negativity of laziness in economic terms: "We accuse our inferiors of laziness . . . but every moment that they take from work is fair revenge for the disproportion they perceive between their pay and the utility of their work." For this author, laziness maintains a balance between "luxury and penury."[8]

But let us return to Rameau, who avoids any instrumentalization of his body and loses himself in pantomime, in the ironic simulation of games of social and political relations. The Nephew's victory over the strategies of power, under the weight of hierarchies, takes place through art, in his canny performance of alienation. He recomposes himself exclusively in this mode, aggrandizing his subaltern status and his noisome beggary. The Nephew thus invents himself a new body abandoned to feelings, to fleeting emotions. Through pantomime, Rameau transforms his servile reality, virtually transfiguring himself through theater and music. Not merely the wretch of his daily misery, he is the ingenious artist of the present. Rameau is a vagabond. His path is laced with alternatives, his parasitism a continual relay race. At home in transition itself, he refuses to pursue any plan, but rather exists in a gyre of pure perambulation.

Devoid of any essential properties, Diderot's Nephew is revealed to us as a series of alterations. He is inconstant, motley, utterly desultory. Diderot has created an alternative character, in unstable equilibrium, restlessly uneven, turbulent (*Nephew*, p. 39). His body is extraordinarily malleable: the text describes him as composite, mixed, mismatched. The musician's defining features are perpetually elusive. The words used to describe him are doubled, alternated, or contradictory (and/and, or/or). The Nephew is a creature in mutation. Likewise his visage (as an expression of personality, a coalescence of character traits, a recognizable individual identity) is sketchy. In its constant variation of expression, it is at times in contradiction not only with the rest of his body but with itself. Rameau, a creature of proliferation, evades the boundaries of the self. He dispenses with the metaphysical anxiety of the *cogito*: "Devil take me if I really know what I am" (p. 79). The Nephew is thus perfectly named in the dialogue: he is referred to as "He" (Lui), with the third person reserved for him alone. He lacks the determinate subjectivity generally associated with the first person personal pronoun. It is useful to recall here the linguistic bias of personology as identified by Gilles Deleuze and Félix Guattari. To the "I" identified as a condition of every utterance, they oppose the indeterminate, indefinite "he" which is susceptible to inchoate events:

> The HE does not represent a subject but rather makes a diagram of an assemblage. It does not overcode statements, it does not transcend them as do the first two persons; on the contrary, it prevents them from falling under the tyranny of subjective or signifying constellations, under the regime of empty redundancies. The contents of the chains of expression it articulates are those that can be assembled for a maximum number of occurrences and becomings. (*A Thousand Plateaus*, p. 265)

The Nephew's pantomime is the exercise of alienation itself, of its infinite permutations.[9] By virtue of playing at everyone else, Rameau is literally *nobody*; at the same time, he is the sum of their masks, which he multiplies ad infinitum.[10] For Diderot, the individual is an actor. He is profoundly adaptable: "At first I watched others at it and did likewise, and even went one better, because I am more downright impudent, a better actor, hungrier and possessed of better lungs" (p. 73). But above all the Nephew is an artist of circumstance, a clever opportunist. Here he describes the variety of his voices:

> [Y]ou must know how to prepare and where to bring in these peremptory tones in the major key, how to seize the occasion and the moment, for example when opinion is divided and the argument has worked itself up to the highest pitch of violence, everybody is talking at once and you can't hear what they are saying. Then you must take up your position some way off in the corner of the room farthest removed from the battlefield, having prepared your explosion by a long silence, and you suddenly drop like a bomb in the middle of the contestants. (*Nephew*, p. 73)

The Nephew's entire body is mobilized to invest in the circumstance, to exploit the adaptability of the moment. Wrested from its form, its rigid, socially defined articulation, it becomes disarticulated, amorphous, polymorphous, extraordinarily fluid:

> I have some soft notes which I accompany with a smile and an infinite variety of approving faces, with nose, mouth, eyes and brow all brought into play. I have a certain agility with my hips, a way of twisting my spine, raising or lowering my shoulders, stretching my fingers, bowing my head, shutting my eyes and being struck dumb as though I had heard an angelic, divine voice come down from heaven. That's what gets them. (p. 74)

Rameau resembles the actor-subject portrayed by Michel Serres in *The Troubadour of Knowledge*. This Harlequin character takes on the multiplicity of others. In fact, he cannot even be charged with wearing masks; rather, he creates living figures in an adaptive theater of intersubjectivity, a prodigious polyphony. He defines himself thus:

> In reality, I am thus all those that I am in and through the successive or juxtaposed relations in which I find myself involved, productive of me, adjectivized subject, subjected to the collective we, and free from myself. . . . Thus the self is a mixed body: studded, spotted, zebrine, tigroid, shimmering, spotted like an ocelot, whose life must be its business. Here Harlequin's coat returns, sewn from adjectives, I mean to say from terms placed side by side.[11]

In dramatic contrast to the orthostatic philosopher (this is the posture maintained throughout the text by the Uncle, the older Rameau who walks straight into the Nephew's panegyric) is our lopsided mime—scruffy, lumpy, deformed, crippled, undone by his habitual contortions: "he seized with his right hand the fingers and wrist of his left and turned them backwards and forwards until his fingertips touched his arm; his joints cracked, and I was afraid that they would be dislocated for good" (pp. 52–53). In his portrait of the Nephew, Diderot might have had in mind the character of Strophios, the pantomime described by Marcel Detienne and Jean-Pierre Vernant in their study of subterfuge in the ancient Greek world. *Strophaîos* is also a term for the sophist, the mobile, supple creature, skilled at "twisting, flexing, interweaving and bending."[12]

In one of the most famous pantomimes of the text, we find the Nephew in a frenzy of multitasking. But his performances are more like kinetic conversions than superimposed images. They go beyond character to tap into feelings, entering the realm of passion. The Nephew's pantomime is noisy, stridently clamorous. The text emphasizes his heterogeneity, the pervasive multiplicity that grabs hold of him and sends him darting every which way. Rameau has become a perfect hodge-podge. Rather than an instrument-body faced with objects to manipulate and integrate, his one-man band is an entire orchestra-body. The pantomime is indeed a sort of pointless gymnastics, an astonishing lack of productivity. In these moments of pure expenditure, Diderot de-composes the body, creating a complex synthesis of delights. He purposefully disorganizes the body, giving it over to the spontaneity of passions, the plasticity of pleasure:

> He sang thirty tunes on top of each other and all mixed up: Italian, French, tragic, comic, of all sorts and descriptions, sometimes in a bass voice going down to the infernal regions, and sometimes bursting himself in a falsetto voice he would split the heavens asunder, taking off the walk, deportment and gestures of the different singing parts. . . . With cheeks puffed out and a hoarse, dark tone he did the horns and bassoons, a bright, nasal tone for the oboes, quickening his voice with incredible agility for the stringed instruments to which he tried to get the closest approximation; he whistled the recorders and cooed the flutes, shouting, singing and throwing himself about like a mad thing: a one-man show featuring dancers, male and female, singers of both sexes, a whole orchestra, a complete opera-house, dividing himself into twenty different stage parts. (pp. 102–103)

Deleuze and Guattari would see Rameau as a "body without organs" that is "permeated by unformed, unstable matters, by flows in all directions, by free intensities" (*A Thousand Plateaus*, p. 40). It is true, as we have seen previously, that the Nephew mentions his lungs—the organ that defines him above all others. But in his case they are a substance, a site for mobilizing affects, a center of nervous excitations, a place where forces are transmitted and exchanged. The lungs obey no particular function here: rather, they are an organ detached from the organism. This organ has adapted to a different metabolic organization of the body; it serves another purpose. These lungs act by agitation, overexcitation, dizzying amplification: "At this point he raised his voice ... 'This,' he went on, 'is where you need lung-power, a powerful organ, plenty of wind'" (p. 104). Here indeed is one of the Nephew's essential characteristics: this expansion of air that makes him an inconsistent, precisely volatile character.

The Genius of the Weak

Diderot's invention of the Nephew refutes the entire ideology of resemblance. His character is never *the same*. It is vicissitude itself, a sort of walking contrariety, a scandal, a monster of dissimilarity: "Nothing is less like him than himself" (p. 34). The Nephew is a hectic, swirling figure who engulfs everything around him. Diderot creates a character in constant flux, eternally off balance, one whose experience of subjectivity is marked by chance, randomness, *circumstance*. The subject in the *Nephew* is caught in a web of positional relations. More precisely, the positions are what define the subject, rather than the other way around. Likewise, the Nephew's parasitism is organized as a fluid compound of fluctuations, an extraordinary mobility of acts and opportunities, of *occasions* (to underline another key term of Diderot's text).

The parasite has no existence but in the open space of circulation: "Somehow or other he had wormed his way into several good homes, where there was always a place laid for him" (p. 35); "Poverty has taught me to make do with anything" (p. 106); "Nothing lasts in this world. Today the top, tomorrow the bottom of the wheel. Bloody circumstances take us along, and take us very badly" (p. 119). Rameau is a sort of gallivanting Harlequin. He must be appreciated above all in the torn, rumpled rags of his patched-up clothing.[13] He is to be admired in his complex meanderings, and in the way he carries with him, on his very person, the memory of his displacements, his *tactical* shifts.

But my use of the term *tactical* requires elaboration. The distinction between tactic and strategy is essential if we wish to understand the virtues of the Nephew's *modus operandi*. A strategy is the result of rational calculation, of a causal and global approach; a tactic, on the other hand, is close to chance: it belongs to the sphere of the random event, the circumstance, the occasion. Michel de Certeau observed the fundamental impropriety of the tactical approach. The tactician always intervenes on the terrain of others. He is devoted to pure exteriority: "This nowhere gives a tactic mobility, to be sure, but a mobility that must accept the chance offerings of the moment, and seize on the wing the possibilities that offer themselves at any given moment."[14] A tactic, he concludes, is "an art of the weak" (*Practice*, p. 37). This is the universe of "clever tricks" and "*coups*," "knowing how to get away with things," of "maneuvers, polymorphic simulations, joyful discoveries" (*Practice*, p. xix).

Rameau tumbles "from one damn thing to another" (p. 119). He is a creature of perennial experimentation. His interlocutor, the philosopher, gives us a quick sketch of this itinerant genius amid his topography of circumstance:

> He lives for the day, gloomy or gay according to circumstances. His first care when he gets up in the morning is to make sure where he will be dining. . . . Night has its own particular worry—whether to tramp home to his little garret. . . , or whether to go to earth in an inn just outside of town. . . . When he has less than six sous in his pocket, which sometimes happens, he falls back on a cabby he knows, or the coachman of some noble lord, who gives him a shake-down on some straw beside his horses. In the morning he still has some of his mattress in his hair. If the weather is mild he walks up and down the Cours or the Champs-Elysées all night. He reappears with the daylight, already dressed yesterday for today and sometimes from today for the rest of the week. (*Nephew*, pp. 34–35)

The champion of the unruly, Rameau is perennially in rebellion against all forms of order or hierarchy. He is a nomad, to use the term as Deleuze understands it: mobilized by the trajectory, he distributes himself in open space through vortical, intensive movement.[15] Rameau refuses to be pinned down. The Nephew's element is transition itself, his movements are a veritable tornado. His parasitism, a succession of stages, traces an unstable, ephemeral geography. Without a plan, he lives in absolute mobility, a hero of the immediate, of calculation on the fly. His space is complicated, crazed with capricious vagaries and catastrophic displacements. Diderot has invented a creature of migration rather than method, of speed rather than sedentarity (as we have seen, his stations are occasional and tactical; the time of his performance is chaotic as opposed to linear). It is no accident that Diderot places his vagabond hero alongside a rather doddering homebody of a philosopher, at once cold and stiff, to whom the Nephew can toss off such assertions as this: "you don't suspect how little the method and the rules matter to me. The man who must have a manual won't ever go far" (p. 76).

A Song in Fugue Form

Another register in which *Rameau's Nephew* develops the dimension of multiplicity is that of music. It offers a new polyphony, one immersed in affect. The tempo of this music is discomposed. Its mode will be rhizomatic, to borrow Deleuze and Guattari's botanical concept contrasting the fixed root with the rhizome's system of ramifications, decenterings, fragmentation, and proliferation:[16] "Nothing is so dull as a succession of common chords. There must be something arresting to break up the beam of light and separate it into rays" (p. 111). The Nephew makes the same demands of lyric art: he wants unpolished phrases, juxtapositions of more condensed, more fragmentary expressions, an accelerated cadence of opposites: "these moments should tumble out quickly one after the other. . . . What we want is exclamations, interjections, suspensions, interruptions, affirmations, negations" (p. 105).

Rameau approaches singing by drawing upon polyvalence and vocal versatility. Through song the voice becomes rhizomatic, in a hybridization of two media, each enhancing the other's potential: "Speech should be thought of as a line, and the tune as another line winding in and out of the first. The more vigorous and true the speech, which is the basis of the tune, and the more closely the tune fits it and the more points of contact it has with it, the truer that tune will be and the more beautiful" (p. 98). For one of his pantomimes the Nephew, in his musical unfolding, chooses the fugue—a series of repetitions, each one fleeing from the others.

To return to my point of departure, the Nephew's idleness: his laziness creates in him a certain relation to non-production, to the unfinished work. The Nephew's brand of production is an invisible repertoire of musical pieces lost to oblivion. He expresses a regret that will find no consolation even in posterity: "I who have composed keyboard pieces which nobody plays, but which may well be the only ones to go down to future generations who will" (p. 48). The philosopher concludes that Rameau has not done anything "worth while" (p. 113). Wistfully he dangles in front of himself the mirage of "a work of art" (p. 114). However, for him the pantomime is a true performance, a work quickened by the instant, and instantaneously liquidated. It is a work that is realized, as his interlocutor remarks, "to no purpose" (p. 54). Witness the sonata that he plays first on the violin, which leaves him "bathed in sweat" (p. 54). His performance is a wonder to behold:

> So there he was, seated at the keyboard, with his legs bent and his head turned ceilingwards, where you would have said he could see a score written out, singing, improvising, playing something by Alberti or Galuppi, I don't know which. His voice went like the wind and his fingers flew over the keys, sometimes abandoning the top part so as to

do the bass, sometimes leaving the accompaniment to take up the top part again. (*Nephew*, p. 54)

The pantomime is a fluid, breezy, ephemeral performance, a product of pure air. It lasts for the duration of transitory passions—once again, a work of volatility.

In this context, it is useful to consider as well the actual person who inspired Diderot, Jean-François Rameau (1716–1777) or, as he signed his own name, Rameau the nephew. In his *Tableau de Paris*, Louis-Sébastien Mercier recounts a conversation between the young Rameau and his father, with the parent's reproaches of heedlessness and sloth, and his expectation of his son's creations: "How long do you expect to live here like this, spineless and idle? For two years I have been waiting for you to produce something."[17] Rameau is known to be the author of compositions for the harpsichord, all of which have been lost. In *La Raméide* (1766), the brilliant self-portrait in poetry in which he sings his own praises and recounts the disappointments of his life—"It seems that heaven created me for setbacks"[18]—here is what Rameau writes about these forgotten works:

> Sous ce titre gravé : *Pièces de clavecin*
> Mes chants ont parcouru ces temples de miracles,
> A plus d'une reprise ont fait acte aux spectacles.
> Tout ce que j'entendis me parût être beau,
> Jusqu'à me prendre alors moi-même pour Rameau.
> Mais pure illusion!
> (*Raméide*, pp. 124–125, lines 20–24)

Under this printed title, *Pieces for Harpsichord*,
My songs have traversed these temples of miracles,
And more than once have witnessed spectacles.
Everything I heard seemed beautiful to me,
So that I even thought myself the real Rameau.
But it was all illusory!

Rameau reverts to the ancestral weight of his musician uncle. The *Raméide* is haunted by the drama of heredity. Here is Rameau's lament:

> Sur les pas de leurs pères
> Voit-on de race en race, également prospères,
> Les aïeux, les germains, les enfants, les neveux
> En partage avoir eu mêmes faveurs des Cieux?
> Dans le rang des talents, si le Ciel n'est propice,
> Le mérite est sans force et dépend du caprice.
> Avant Rameau peut-être on aurait pu me voir
> Paraître avec éclat dans le rang du savoir.
> Tout dépend ici-bas du temps, des circonstances.
> *(Raméide*, p. 125, lines 25–33)

> Looking from clan to clan, do we observe
> Elders, cousins, children and nephews
> Tracing their fathers' footsteps and flourishing alike,
> All equally endowed with Heaven's gifts?
> In the ranking of talents, without the Heavens' favor,
> Merit is helpless and depends on chance.
> Before Rameau, perhaps, one might have seen
> Me shining in the pantheon of knowledge.
> Here on earth it all depends on time and circumstance.

Diderot suggests an equally original interpretation of this genealogical drama, as voiced by the Nephew. The hereditary failure, according to the Nephew's explanation, is a parodic reprise of the ancestral model, a toxic rictus of nature, the grimace of transmission: "[Nature] took on a solemn and imposing look when she formed dear uncle Rameau. . . . When she botched up his nephew she made a face, and then another face and then yet another" (pp. 113–114).

Jacques Cazotte, who composed a *Nouvelle Raméide* as a follow-up to Rameau's autobiographical poem, replays the artist's Oedipal dilemma. Jesting about Rameau's "indolence," he reports the Uncle's commandment: "Mon neveu, comme un diable il vous faut travailler, / Et d'estoc et de taille il vous faut ferrailler" ("My nephew, you must work like the devil, / Cutting and thrusting with your sword").[19] But Cazotte immediately points to the Nephew's unharnessed talent and his unfinished, ephemeral work. The young Rameau's art is an impromptu art of the moment. It is the genius of quips and unexpected strokes:

> This character, a born musician, perhaps even more so than his uncle, was never able to plumb the depths of his art; but he was born filled with song, and he had the uncanny ability to find agreeable and expressive songs in impromptu fashion, from a few words that one might suggest to him; but it would have taken a true artist to arrange and correct his phrases, and to compose the scores. (Cited in *Rameau le neveu*, p. 221)

In any case, these "musical sallies" constitute a deeply ironic body of work, as can be seen in the titles of some of these pieces, the moral portraits that he created for the harpsichord: the *Magnifiques*, the *Persifleurs* (*The Banterers*), the *Gens du bon ton* (*People of Good Taste*), the *Petits-Maîtres* (*The Fops*), the *Encyclopédie*.[20]

Rameau the unproductive artist is indeed genuinely *désœuvré*, literally workless. He is a true artist of "infamy," in the precise sense given to the term by the art critic Jean-Yves Jouannais: "everything that, intentionally or not, opposes, even condemns, notoriety, renown, glory, *fama*."[21] By contrast, the divine Uncle, the Great Rameau, is the man of works, of *opera*, in both the etymological and the musical senses of the term. In Diderot's dialogue, Rameau the Nephew is constantly invoking the Uncle's works like a running sum. In *La Raméide*, Rameau the nephew ticks off the bitter count: "*Hippolyte, Castor, les Indes, Dardanus, / Zoroastre, Trajan, Pygmalion et plus!*" (*Raméide*, p. 127, lines 123–124). It is as if the Uncle had exhausted all possible musical material. Likewise, the treatises written by the uncle (these numerous methodical works, writings of Cartesian mathematical inspiration, include *Traité de l'harmonie* [*Treatise on Harmony*]; *Nouveau système de musique théorique* [*New System of Theoretical Music*]; and *Traité de musique théorique* [*Treatise on theoretical music*]) cause Rameau to lament:

> Il semble avoir dit seul dans son heureux délire:
> "A nos derniers neveux ne laissons rien à dire!"
> ... Comment puis-je à l'aspect du plus petit volume,
> Sensément me résoudre à prendre en main la plume?
> (*Raméide*, p. 127, lines 121–122, 125–126)

> He seems to have said, alone in his blithe delirium:
> "Let us leave nothing for our last nephews to say!"
> ... How in my right mind, with the least volume in view,
> Can I resolve to take my quill in hand?

Next to his uncle's output, the Nephew's meager musical and vocal fragments are destined for erasure—a few vaudeville verses eroded by oblivion. Rameau the Nephew seems doomed to "obscurity" (*Raméide*, p. 125, line 35 and p. 126, line 65). Diderot's text condemns him as an eternal "scraper of strings" (*Nephew*, p. 109).

All in all, the Nephew's laziness could be read as a classic Œdipal reaction to the ultimate work: that of heredity, of biological accomplishment.[22] The Nephew coasts along in reverie, the ultimate act of non-production, in creative suspension; in a dream he conjures his creation, projected vicariously through a prolific uncle, in a hypnotic appropriation of the work: "What's up with you, Rameau? You're dreaming. And what are you dreaming about? That you have done or are doing something to spark the admiration of the universe" (*Nephew*, p. 116).

The Nephew can be placed within the peculiar genealogy of the present study, which began with Marivaux's journalist and his Indigent Philosopher, even more closely akin to the Nephew. Diderot brilliantly exploits the oppositional dimension of laziness that we have already observed in Marivaux. Like his predecessors,

Diderot's character also makes the insolent choice of fragmentation in preference to the unified whole. The Nephew composes in the same turbulence; he shares the same flighty physiology. Diderot pushes this volatility to its very limits: the absence of completion. Diderot's flâneur-musician tosses aside the finished work as readily as his Marivaudian predecessor.

As for Jean-François Rameau, he was to finish out his days in a hospital run by the Bons-Fils d'Armentières, where he was saddled with a whole array of marginalizing diagnoses: insanity, "public nuisance,"[23] "extreme destitution."[24] Also mentioned is the "incapacitating fatigue"[25] that seems to have overtaken him. These lines from the *Raméide* are telling:

> En naissant l'on n'a rien ou l'on est héritier;
> L'un doit vivre du sien et l'autre d'un métier.
> Voilà comme aujourd'hui j'entends encore la thèse.
> Combien comme héritiers je vois paraître à l'aise,
> Quand il faut chaque jour m'armer d'un nouveau soin
> Pour aller malgré moi combattre le besoin!
> (*Raméide*, p. 131, lines 7–12)

Some are born broke, others inherit wealth;
Some live off their own and others from a trade.
This is the way things still appear to me.
How many I see take their ease like heirs,
When every day I have to shoulder fresh cares
To combat hard necessity despite myself.

Good night, Rameau!

Portrait of the Philosopher in Rags

In return for a favor he performed for a certain Madame Geoffrin, Diderot receives a burdensome gift: a new dressing gown. His benefactor's well-intended gesture does not stop there, but ends up transforming Diderot's entire study: the furniture and accessories are replaced and, in spite of himself, Diderot is forced to make a fresh start. His nostalgic lamentations over the discarded garment were to find lasting fame in his essay, "Regrets on Parting With My Old Dressing Gown" (1769). This "fragment," in which Diderot blushes at the opulence of his new gown, superimposes two images of the writer. Written while he recovered from his encyclopedic exertions, this brief text bears the marks of a depressive suspension of work: "Every morning, when I get up, I feel disgust, numbness, aversion to ink, pens, and books, which betoken either laziness or else obsolescence."[26]

What Diderot highlights in this text, through a largely mythical image of the writer at work, is the writer's profession itself, his social status. Fleshing out the construction of this image is the following portrait of Diderot in his old dressing gown found in one of his letters to Sophie Volland:

> My taste for solitude grows by the minute. Yesterday I went out in my dressing gown and nightcap to dine at d'Amilaville's. I can no longer abide street clothes. My beard grows as much as it wants. Another month of this sedentary life, and I'll be more of a hermit than the deserts of St. Pachomius have ever seen.[27]

The famous gown makes another appearance in these same letters, where Diderot claims he has grown used to his "surpeau" (second skin).[28] This second instance emphasizes the philosopher's penchant "for study and retreat" (*Correspondance*, v. 5, p. 213): "The dressing gown persists more than ever. More than ever I like my cabinet and my books" (*Lettres à Sophie Volland*, p. 291). Elsewhere Diderot confesses his wish never to "remove his dressing gown" (*Correspondance*, v. 5, p. 178). The philosopher's retreat progressively shrinks until it is virtually coterminous with his person.

In Diderot's "Regrets," the old gown is identified with that marginal philosophical figure, the cynic. Here the nostalgic allusion to Diogenes is key. This "little paper,"[29] as Melchior Grimm referred to the essay, also wrestles with the value of *otium* in its aristocratic form. The new scarlet gown, Diderot tells us, is not suited to the pensive philosopher, but rather made to clothe a "rich loafer."[30] The philosopher's activity cannot be compared to the idleness of the rich.

Diderot thus wishes to retire to his familiar universe, the private disorder of his dusty study. The old dressing gown was polyvalent, serving many purposes: "it used to lend itself complaisantly to any demand I chose to make on it, for the poor are almost always quick to be of service" ("Regrets," p. 309). Not only was the old gown a second skin—"It draped itself so snugly, yet loosely, around all the curves and angles of my body" ("Regrets," p. 309)—but it was adapted to the elements: "Neither did I have to watch out for flying sparks from the fire or for water leaking in through the roof" ("Regrets," p. 309).

The clothes, then, did more than make the man: the cloth was a written page, covered with impressions. The discarded gown, marked by signs tracing the flow of words, was a palimpsest: "If the ink was too thick and refused to run out of my pen—presto, there was the skirt of my old dressing gown ready to serve as a penwiper. You could see how many times it had done me this service by the long, black stripes it bore. Those stripes were the badge of an author, . . . evidence that I am an honest workman" ("Regrets," p. 309). The old gown bore all the stigmata of intellectual labor. It was the extension of the crafted page, a *tabula maculata*. Exchanging the old gown for the new, the philosopher is thus stripped of his mnemonic comforter. Now the unfamiliar trappings wrap him in worry. This scene is reminiscent of an episode in Diderot's *Rameau's Nephew*, an awkward exchange between the philosopher and the Nephew. Rameau, himself "in . . . ragged breeches, tattered" (p. 34), reminds the philosopher of a time when he was not so well-heeled. Displayed before his eyes is a paltry article of clothing: "a shaggy grey coat. . . . Threadbare on one side, with a frayed cuff, and black woollen stockings darned up the back with white thread" (p. 55; translation modified). Another time, a bygone life. . . .

The terms in which Diderot's "Regrets" evokes false riches, obscene opulence, and artifice incline to indigence. Identifying with penurious marginality, the philosopher wishes to forget the "precious garment," celebrating instead the "piece of ordinary cloth" ("Regrets," p. 310). Let us accompany Diderot on his upsetting survey of the renovated space: the philosopher's cabinet, post-makeover. The entire study suffers the "ravages Luxury has made" ("Regrets," p. 310). He laments the loss of other "rags" that he has been divested of. His den of indigence was once a floor-to-ceiling space of cozy disorder: "A chair made out of woven straw, a rough wooden table, a cheap Bergamo tapestry, a pine board that served for a bookshelf, a few grimy engravings without frames, tacked by the corners to the tapestry, and three or four plaster casts that hung between the engravings" ("Regrets," pp. 310–311). This is the squalid den he misses, the dwelling of the philosopher. It recalls the poor man's garret described in *Rameau's Nephew*. Diderot takes stock of the newly luxurious study: precious desk, inlaid armoire, leather armchair, a large mirror to decorate the mantelpiece, a gold clock, damask drapes. The philosopher's study has been transformed into a financier's cabinet, the office of a royal tax collector. The philosopher is no longer recognizable. Rather, Diderot shows us the "rich loafer" mentioned earlier (p. 309).

Louis-Sébastien Mercier described the mythical space of the study in similar terms. In *Mon bonnet de nuit* (*My Nightcap*), not only is the image of the philosopher's asylum a snapshot of chaos, with papers cluttered in comfortable confusion, but its occupant is custom-made for his surroundings. The section entitled "Le galetas littéraire" ("The Literary Hovel") depicts the philosopher as a Harlequin figure in a patchy costume, a tattered dressing gown of moth-eaten fabric, threadbare from use. Mercier, like Diderot,

extols this proud penury, the lofty refuge that shelters the philosopher from the concerns of the rich.[31]

Clearly Diderot is shaken up by Madame Geoffrin's overhaul
of his home. He cannot help but miss the distressed arrangement
that was so congenial to his customary laziness:

> The wooden table still held its ground, protected as it was
> by a great heap of pamphlets and loose papers piled up
> helter-skelter. This encumbrance seemed likely to preserve
> it in safety for many a long day from the humiliation that
> threatened to descend upon it. But notwithstanding my
> natural laziness, Fate at last worked its will with my table:
> the papers and pamphlets are now neatly stacked in the
> drawers of an expensive new desk. ("Regrets," p. 312)

The extravagant refurbishing leaves Diderot unsettled. The
new scarlet gown is described as a parasite, an alien intruder. The
only concession the writer's new environment makes to the old:
"an old braided carpet" ("Regrets," p. 313), which must remind
him of his old rags, his erstwhile retreat. He clings to this scrap of
his former abode. Trampling this "pitiable" rug ("Regrets," p. 313)
underfoot, he can remember his former indigence, perpetuate the
myth of mediocrity, and picture beneath the magnificent garment
the humble philosopher like the peasant in his hut. The philosopher would like to preserve forever this foothold of humility, this
beggarly ground.

In his remarks on a portrait by Louis-Michel Van Loo that was
exhibited at the Salon of 1767, Diderot had already reflected on
the luxurious dressing gown which clashed with the idealized image of the "impoverished writer" (figure 6). Diderot bemoaned the
fact that this painting did not show the philosopher in meditation, his mental efforts manifest in an air of reverie: "Then his lips
would be parted, his gaze fixed far away, and the labor inside his
exceedingly busy head would be painted upon his face."[32] In contrast, the proper posture was indeed captured, or as Diderot says

Figure 6. Louis-Michel Van Loo, *Denis Diderot* (1767).
Oil on canvas, 81 x 65 cm. Musée du Louvre, Paris.
Photo: Erich Lessing/Art Resource, NY.

"seized," by another painter, Garand. In a letter to Sophie Volland, Diderot describes this other portrait's rarely encountered degree of resemblance. Here the sage is presented in perfectly appropriate attire. The portraitist has succeeded in rendering the mental effort, the instant of meditation:

I am portrayed bareheaded, in my dressing gown, sitting in an armchair, my right arm supporting my left, which in turn cradles my head, my collar in disarray, my eyes with a far-off look, like someone who is meditating. Indeed, in this painting I *am* meditating, I live and breathe, I am full of life; the thinking shows through the forehead. (*Œuvres esthétiques*, p. 512)

In the redecorated interior, one final substitution does prove a boon to the philosopher. The writer welcomes into his home the supreme artist: the painter. Out of its entire congeries of objects and opulent furniture, the apartment has only one thing to recommend itself to the beholder: a painting by Vernet. "It is to admire Vernet that they come to my house. The artist has humbled the philosopher" ("Regrets," p. 316 [translation modified]). The painting restores the study's hospitality along with its good taste. Through the roundabout of a tumultuous rearrangement, art has resumed its place in the order of things, keeping a distance from the seductions of wealth. The strips of writing described nostalgically at the beginning of Diderot's essay end up recycled by the painter's palette in the description of Vernet's *Tempest*.

The "Regrets" disdained the artificial harmony of luxurious objects. Here the only true harmony is restored, that which is born of light and shadow, which is created only by the rarest of techniques. Vernet's *Tempest*, a tableau after Diderot's heart, paints the circumstances of a passing instant, the elements poised at the brink of catastrophe: turbulent sea, uncertain weather, sky and waves in turmoil. Diderot and Vernet speak the same meteorological language. The philosopher's roof becomes the painter's house—thus the enthusiastic invitation that concludes the text: "Come see my Vernet..." ("Regrets," p. 317).

The opposite takes place in Baudelaire's "La Chambre double," one of the *petits poèmes en prose* in his *Spleen de Paris*. This time it is the imagination that transforms the poet's apartment into the locus of the beautiful, through the rule of harmony: "Sur les murs nulle abomination artistique" ("No artistic abomination on the walls").[33] The writer's hovel becomes a "*spirituelle*" (*spiritual*; p. 280) room. But the dream is quickly dashed, and the poet's garret subsides into its ordinary squalor, its everyday filth. Then the weight of life resumes, the display of unfinished work, the dispirited fantasmagoria: "Voici les meubles sots, poudreux, écornés; la cheminée sans flamme et sans braise . . . les manuscrits, raturés ou incomplets" ("Look at the stupid furniture, dusty and chipped; the hearth devoid of fire and embers . . . the manuscripts, crossed out or incomplete"; p. 280). The room of dreams is actually a space of laziness, of slow motion: the subject is as if paralyzed, the very objects enveloped in a similar apathy. The whole spiritual room is half asleep: "Les meubles ont l'air de rêver; on les dirait doués d'une vie somnambulique" ("The furniture seems to be dreaming, as if living in a state of trance"; p. 280). But in the end, time's whip cracks the spell, and the impulse to work rushes back with the terrible force of a commandment: "Et hue donc! bourrique! Sue donc esclave! Vis donc, damné!" ("Get a move on, donkey! Sweat, slave! Live, doomed soul!"; p. 282).

[5]

Philosophy on the Pillow

Joubert

Diderot is fond of his dressing gown. The writer's study is an extension of his nighttime cocoon, where moments of creativity take the slippered philosopher by surprise. This is the same space that Louis-Sébastien Mercier, already known for his *Tableau de Paris*, conjures up in *Mon Bonnet de nuit* (*My Nightcap*), an anthology of his midnight musings. Here scraps of paper are pieced together during the respite from the daily hubbub. Before entering into the realm of sleep, the writer welcomes the final ruminations of his waking hours. These are the thoughts that will accompany him to bed: "How sweet it is, alone in one's nightcap, to converse with the tip of one's quill! One is master of his ideas and expressions; one fashions his thoughts in his own way; one is oblivious to critics and purists; one writes copiously, and not without sensual pleasure" (*Mon bonnet*, p. 11).

In such an instant Mercier discovers a taste of freedom, of liberation from all constraints. The writer, close by his pillow, is reconciled to the pleasure of writing, and his pen is freed from the judgment of others, from the hold of the public. Nocturnal thought, closing out the day's turbulence and criticism, brings rest to the writer: "one has written what one wished, unbridled and unchecked. After that, the public may voice its opinion. Each has been free; each can count his own pleasure" (*Mon bonnet*, p. 13). Thus the writer escapes the moral debt that can bind him to the public. The pillow of sleep provides the pleasure of self-satisfaction: "How sweet it is to tell oneself, one's head cradled on the pillow: I have fulfilled my vocation, and when I give the public much more than I receive from them, they are in my debt . . . they are collectively beholden to me, but I am not to them. I have provided them with enjoyable sensations, and what could they add to those that I have felt in writing?" (*Mon bonnet*, p. 13).

Mercier will return to his liberating pillow to explain how the night favors philosophy. It is the ideal time for contemplation: suspending the frenzy of the day, it fosters the peaceful circulation of ideas. The head resting on the pillow releases a particular form of leisure, a happy provocation of consciousness. The writer's very work takes on a new dimension as it becomes accustomed to repose:

> The night is the common benefactor of all that breathes: it is during its reign that the greatest sum of happiness is spread over the earth: violent passions are interrupted, crushing labors no longer exhaust the human race . . . Oh night! lay down once again for me your silent hours; nourish my peaceful work, and let my paper flow with the feelings and ideas that gratify my contemplative soul! (*Mon bonnet*, pp. 286–287)

Scattered through Mercier's *Bonnet de nuit* are dreams or "celestial" reveries, as he calls them, meditations in which the spirit levitates, absconds from "solid" reality. These aerial dreams can produce flights of mind unbound by human gravity, moments of utopia wrested from social and political violence. The solitary study welcomes the dream state that would forget murder and injustice: "Suddenly cannon fire startles me awake. . . . And me, fleeing the tumult of public rejoicings, the noise of burning saltpeter, the drunkenness of the blinded masses, I escaped the mob" (*Mon bonnet*, p. 92). At night the philosopher is in his element. The musing spirit of *Mon bonnet de nuit* presents a marked contrast with Mercier's grand *opus*, the encyclopedic *Tableau de Paris*, which he confesses has been written with the sheer force of his "legs," mim-

ing the speed and frenzy of the city he is describing, in his effort
to "to see it all."[1]

Another insomniac was Joseph Joubert, a friend of Diderot's
and an admirer of Mercier. Certain pages of Joubert's *Carnets*
(*Notebooks*) read as pastiches or summaries of Mercier's *Tableau de
Paris*. Of course Joubert was never to write a book. Maurice Blanchot, who devotes a fascinating chapter of *Le Livre à venir* (*The
Book to Come*) to Joubert, explores the enigma of this writer who
kept company with "prolific men of letters"[2] and wrote nonstop
but published nothing. "Why doesn't Joubert write books?" (p.
52), Blanchot asks—despite the fact that he is endowed with "the
gift of that century" (p. 52), all the requisite talents of expression.
The *Carnets*, Joubert's journals, collect his abundant thoughts,
ranging from 1774 to 1824, the year of his death.

The editor of the *Carnets*, André Beaunier, mentions Joubert's
laziness when it came to writing, despite the continuous activity of his mind. Joubert himself distinguishes different classes of
laziness, varieties of idleness: "There are lazy heads and there are
lazy bodies, apathies and indolence of movement, incapacities of
care, concern, and attention, and lacks of activity."[3] Beaunier also
describes Joubert as a homebody, bundled up against the dreaded
cold, with multiple layers covering his head. He paints this portrait
of the retiring writer:

> Moreover he has a thick muffler around his neck and
> shoulders which cascades down his narrow chest. Over
> his sparse head of hair, he would sport, at the least hint of
> a cold, an embarrassment of headgear. . . . He took pains
> over his outer layers, and chose the brown nankeen of his
> frock coats with no more frivolity than he applied to the
> selection of his overcoats, woollen stockings, slippers, and
> quilted sleeves. (*Carnets*, Preface, p. 8)

As he aged, Joubert, coiffed in his ever-present cap, kept to his
bed and insisted on his precious "rest." Beaunier cites one of the

writer's friends, Madame de Chastenay, who finds him "tucked into his bed almost like a woman in confinement" with "a large cotton cap."[4] The bed, after all, is not in the least incompatible with the writer's creative burgeoning. Thought flourishes in horizontal comfort: "The bed's warmth during the day. The ferment it provokes (in the mind)" (*Carnets*, 2: 618). Joubert himself claims to have "a tender mind and character: I require the temperature of the gentlest coddling" (*Carnets*, 1: 343). In a letter to Madame de Vintimille, he mentions his laziness "that has become incurable by virtue of being chronic."[5] This laziness, however, is not part of any campaign; it does not lend itself to an ethical agenda. In this regard, it differs from Rousseau's laziness, which Joubert judges severely: "life without action, nothing but feelings and half-sensual thoughts, pretentious *far niente*, pleasurable cowardice, futile and lazy activity that fattens the soul without improving it" (*Carnets*, 2: 716). Joubert's laziness is, in a word, ontological; it is an inability to bring work to completion, a primordial worklessness: he is, he notes succinctly, "incapable of work" (*Carnets* 2: 628). His brand of *otium* is truly negative, without will. Joubert is quite simply the artist of the unfinished: sketches for an *Eloge de Cook* (*In Praise of Cook*), preliminary notes for books, an *Histoire impartiale de la France* (*An Impartial History of France*)—none of these volumes would ever reach maturity. Blanchot succinctly sums up the peculiar destiny of this "author without a book . . . and writer without writing" (*The Book To Come*, p. 54). In the end, Joubert's work tends toward the "white book" over which he agonized, the impossible, perfect book that would be torture to finish. But he achieves acceptance: "My mind is not my master, nor am I master of myself: he is absent and I don't know what to tell you" (*Carnets*, 1: 371).

Blanchot justly saw Joubert as the writer par excellence of the book to come. He had envisioned this mythical, hidden, secret book, a project that was impossible to begin and to finish, without any conclusion—doomed from the outset to disappearance. For Joubert, publication was always something to be put off until the next time. His autobiography begins with a phrase that perfectly expresses the context of this non-production: "For a long time I have withstood the torments of a fertility that cannot bring itself into the open" (*Carnets*, 2: 539). And Blanchot—flouting those who would cast Joubert as a moralist with his pronouncements unfurled for all eternity—insists on reading him instead as a writer of the ephemeral, the day-to-day. For Blanchot, this is the locus of Joubert's enigmatic modernity: "What he wrote he wrote almost every day, dating it and not giving it any remarkable reference point other than this date, or any other perspective besides the movement of the days that had brought it to him" (*The Book*, p. 50). This view of the *Carnets* is echoed by Pierre Pachet, who sees them as defined by a successiveness in which they are inscribed as events.[6] But Blanchot himself, removing these pages from their everyday epiphany, immediately adds this nuance: "If his *Journal* is still grounded in the days, it is not a reflection of them, but instead strives for something beyond them" (*The Book*, p. 53).

Let us now enter into these *Carnets*, this collection of diurnal thoughts or mental snapshots. Joubert's work is haunted by incompleteness. He writes: "Conclude! What a word. One does not conclude when one stops and declares oneself finished" (*Carnets*, 2: 647). His first attempt to produce a finished work did not pan out. For this project, suggested by Diderot and entitled "La Bienveillance universelle" ("Universal Good Will"), Joubert admits that "the material was lacking" (*Carnets*, 1: 433). This awareness would continually hound Joubert's efforts. Moreover, he detested making detailed plans, which marred the pleasure of writing. A plan serves primarily for mechanically written books, those constructed with foresight. Incompleteness not only highlights the element of chance, of newness, but it also puts the artist's pleasure first:

> To make a precise and detailed plan in advance is to deprive
> one's mind of all the pleasures of discovery and of novelty

in the execution of the work. It is to make that execution insipid for oneself and therefore impossible in works that exclude enthusiasm and imagination. Such a plan is itself a half-work. It must be left imperfect if one is to derive any pleasure. One must tell oneself that it should not be completed. (*Carnets*, 1: 170)

Orderly progression repels Joubert. When he thinks of succession, he turns to music for his model: "Thoughts must follow one another and intertwine, like the sounds of music—harmony—and not like the links in a chain or pearls on a string" (*Carnets*, 1: 320). He shies away from order, from Cartesian linearity. If, as he says, "the mind loves order" (*Carnets*, 2: 700), he nevertheless wishes to invent an order that would not be compromised by any constraint or straitened by inflexible rectitude: "Literary and poetic order depends on the natural and free succession of movements" (*Carnets*, 2: 700). Further, Joubert's aesthetics do not exclude a "beautiful disorder" (*Carnets*, 2: 785). Instead of rigid alignment, Joubert chooses fluidity, fluency, flux. He offers this stylistic advice, no doubt with his model Montaigne in mind: ("[Language] must have cadence or emotion, abandon, effusiveness, streaming and flooding (floating) so to speak, like the clouds in the air. Rippling, billowing style" (*Carnets*, 1: 152). In other words: "To speak through waves, through swells of water" (*Carnets*, 2: 541). Joubert protests against unwavering consistency of style, against unbroken succession, for "In the soul, all is spurt and interruption" (*Carnets*, 1: 463).

Another of Joubert's thoughts emphasizes the benefit of the random, the unforeseen: "But how can one look where one ought when one doesn't even know what one is looking for? And that is what always happens when one composes and when one creates. Fortunately, straying in this way, one makes more than a discovery, one has fortunate encounters" (*Carnets*, 2: 648). Like Diderot, Joubert is a circumstantial thinker. His thought is meteorological, at the mercy of the elements. Rejecting the plan and method of Cartesian rule, Joubert finds Descartes "too mechanical for his taste" (*Carnets*, 1: 316). He willingly denounces Descartes's statics, his geometric reduction "through figure and movement," the famous "fixed point" that organizes both his space and his doctrine. In sum: "Adieu, Descartes!" (*Carnets*, 1: 314). Thinking of the philosopher's machine-universe, Joubert labels him "the greatest automatist in the world" (*Carnets*, 1: 316). He explains how mathematical rationality represents reality, by smoothing rough edges, by idealizing and flattening the real:

> Mathematics deals only with semi-abstractions, for it operates on mere shadows of realities: the line is the shadow of a thread or of a taut hair, the point is the shadow of a nib, the circle is the shadow of a hoop. Just as one detaches these terminal figures from flat objects in order to reveal the figures alone to our eyes, likewise, through abstraction, one detaches from realities the qualities or properties brought to bear in them, in order to expose these qualities alone to the mind that considers them. (*Carnets*, 1: 242)

Joubert prefers a less certain medium—the air which he so often describes, the winds whose gusts he yields to:

> Whoever lives in uncertain times, however firm and un-flagging in his principles, he cannot be so in all their applications; though firm in his plans, in his step he will be unable always to keep either to the same resolutions or to the same paths. He must abandon certain parts of himself to the winds (that is, to circumstances). I would liken him to those giant trees, the walnut trees whose branches sway back and forth in the storm, bending and bowing above, below, right, left, shaking in every leaf although their trunks remain immobile. In this comparison there is an image of myself that pleases me, for it excuses, by explaining

them to me, some variations that I dislike in both myself and others. (*Carnets*, 2: 928)

It is no surprise that Joubert's writing found its most apt expression in the genre of brief notation, of the fragment. He writes decisively: "Like Montaigne, I am 'unsuited to continuous discourse'" (*Carnets*, 2: 638). He practices "the genius of brevity" (*Carnets*, 1: 435). The long haul is not his strong suit: he quickly loses interest. His paramount practice is that of *scribbling*. Returning to his famous notebooks, Joubert is incapable of taking up where he left off. He immediately falters, defeated by boredom or fatigue, and confesses:

I have just spent two weeks poring over my old papers, which were stored in packets that had been sewn shut a dozen years ago. There I found scribblings that I had forgotten more than twenty years ago. All this made me fairly disgusted with myself, and I am quite relieved to be rid of the lot. My exhaustion from this task, combined with great boredom, has truly overwhelmed me.[7]

In the *Carnets*, we see that Joubert has not given up his search for the subtle, for what is detached from solid matter or weight. He is a strict spiritualist, a staunch exponent of spirit. In his cultivation of the spirit, Joubert detaches himself from matter, distancing himself as far as possible from the solid world in favor of a world where things are liquid. His is a physics of the gaseous, where things float in a state of evaporation. Joubert shares Marivaux's predilection for air and water. His world is a volatile aggregate of bubbles, an ephemeral concretion of vapors. Upon examination, even Joubert's solidity reveals itself to be only air: "This globe is a drop of water; the world is a drop of air. Marble is air made dense" (*Carnets*, 1: 468). In another fragment of the *Carnets*, Joubert describes the earth in terms of all its corpuscular, liquid elements. Far from a solid globe, it is a truly aerial body: "The earth is a globe sprinkled with a little dust, traversed by a few streams of water and suspended in the atmosphere like all the other stars" (*Carnets*, 1: 149). Joubert's matter verges on immateriality—his famous "appearance," to which I shall return below. He will explain the liquefaction of things by emphasizing this fact of matter, its constituent "tenuousness" (*Carnets*, 1: 235). He repeats elsewhere: "The world is a drop of air" (*Carnets*, 2: 730).

Conceiving of an anti-Newtonian, chemical universe, Joubert distances himself radically from classical deterministic mechanics, from science tethered to the law of gravity. A notation in the *Carnets* shows his view of the Newtonian universe as one of compulsive measurement, of mathematical abstraction: "Newton. He was endowed with the capacity to quantify everything" (*Carnets*, 2: 307). Challenging the universality of Newton's system, Joubert compares the scientist to an accountant: "Newton. It is no more true that he discovered the system of the world, than it is true that whoever made a fair copy of the administration's accounts discovered a system of government" (*Carnets*, 1: 186). And again: "Newton's only invention was how much" (*Carnets*, 1: 313). The law of gravity is subject to the same criticism, and Joubert offers an alternative theory which perceives a world that is closer to turbulence, to a whirlwind of movement. The world, Joubert observes, is a "tourbillon" (vortex; *Carnets*, 1: 143) that induces vertigo. His is a different view of the cosmological displacement of bodies:

> Don't you say that the force of gravity carries bodies from high to low? —Yes. —And that the path traced by weighty falling bodies is a straight line? —True. —Then imagine another force, whether simple or complex, which causes bodies to whirl and in whirling to trace the shape of an egg or an O. . . . There is in nature a force of whirling just as there is a force of gravity. (*Carnets*, 1: 193)

Joubert generalizes this force as an inexorable physical law: "Whirling: produced by the rush of air in windmills; by the rush of water in watermills; by the breath, in short, in all cases, in all materials" (*Carnets*, 1: 239).

Joubert likes the random chaos of the cloud. Michel Serres, seeing the cloud as the repressed of the history of science, writes of this exclusion: "As soon as modern physics formulates, by shapes and movements, by quantitative and controlled experimentation in closed sub-systems, it abandons the phenomena which resist its abstraction to contemptible minor trades."[8] Just what sort of object is the cloud? For the Lucretian philosopher, the cloud is primary, formed "by the flow, waves of vapour, rivers of wind. Amorphous gathering of certain currents emanating from the earth and the water" (*The Birth of Physics*, p. 87). In addition to clouds, Joubert is attracted to other forms of what Serres calls "concepts for multiplicities":[9] fire and flame flare up everywhere in the *Carnets*.

In this sense, Joubert remains close to his first master, Diderot. Here is a corpuscular physics that opposes the solid, the full, the dense concretion. The bubble-universe has a horror of the hard: "Yes, the world is made of gauze, a transparent gauze even. Newton calculated that a diamond had much more empty space than full, and the diamond is the most compact of bodies" (*Carnets*, 1: 466). For Joubert, the diamond—of all stones ranked as the paragon of rigidity—loses all its hardness, its noble solidity; it becomes "a bit of luminous mud" (*Carnets*, 1: 161). Or rather, in yet another rejection of the universe of weight and gravity:

> With its gravitations, its impenetrabilities, its attractions, its impulsions, and all the blind forces so loudly trumpeted by scientists..., what is all of matter, but an emptied grain of metal, a hollowed-out grain of glass, a ballooning water bubble upon which light and dark play; in short a shadow where nothing weighs except upon itself, nothing is impenetrable except to itself. (*Carnets*, 2: 906)

Joubert reiterates his vision of a porous world of hollow objects: "The whole world is but gauze. Even iron in its porousness is no more than crepe paper" (*Carnets*, 1: 162). "Everything is hollow; and the elements themselves are hollow" (*Carnets*, 1: 146). Joubert is the physicist of intermittence. He sees the world fluctuating between empty and full. He suffocates in the face of Cartesian fullness: "Everything is so full in this system that there is no time or place for thought itself. One is always tempted to cry out as if in the theatre stalls: *We need air, air! Space!*" (*Carnets*, 1: 241). Joubert does not even believe in complete fullness, which he splits apart with interstices. Fullness is an abstraction. Joubert reveals it as pierced, fissured, intermittent space: "Fullness is nothing but a big sponge. If one squeezed it, if one got rid of the empty space, it would not amount to a handful. Fluid is a vapor that could be reduced to a drop; a cloud, a work of mesh is an image of fullness" (*Carnets*, 1: 232–233). Joubert's space is tattered, and when he imagines his work, he is pursuing the same idea of the aerated tableau, crazed with intervals, diffuse: "I would like thoughts to succeed one another in a book like stars in the sky, with order and harmony, but relaxed and dispersed, without touching, without merging . . . Yes, I would like them to mill around without catching or sticking together, so that each one of them could subsist on its own" (*Carnets*, 1: 263). Joubert's idea, and above all its epiphany, are conceived in this aerial element: "our most subtle ideas are formed by evaporation" (*Carnets*, 1: 272). The fractal state in which he left us his work is entirely consistent with his theory: the papers, thoughts, bundles and leaves form an inscription of the vacant and the intermittent, placed in time's path of no return.

The Spirit of the Cloud

Let us return to Joubert's spiritualism. It is no surprise to find his work imbued with the primacy of the soul. Its immateriality is described in atmospheric terms: "It is a fiery vapor which burns without being consumed. . . . The flame of this vapor is not only light, but feeling" (*Carnets*, 1: 107).[10] Whence the imperative—"To give soul to things, to words, to lines" (*Carnets*, 1: 621)—that governs all of Joubert's rhetoric. In this sense, thought is ordered in relation to the soul, partaking of the same matter: "Thought forms in the soul like clouds in the air" (*Carnets*, 1: 64).

The word *subtle* alone would suffice to describe Joubert's version of matter. In fact, the subtle is ascendant for him. It preempts the solid and conditions the weighty: "Observe that everywhere and in everything, what is subtle carries that which is compact, and what is light holds suspended all that is heavy" (cited by Blanchot, *The Book*, pp. 57–58). In a text written October 19, 1821, in one of the "chapters" written toward the end of Joubert's life with a view to explaining his philosophical thoughts, we see one of the most spiritualist developments of the idea of matter:

> I have said and I was right: matter is an appearance. Everything is little and nothing is a lot. For in fact, what is the world and what is the whole world? The whole world, if we look closely, is but a bit of condensed ether, ether is but a bit of space, and space is but a point that was endowed with the capacity to spread out a bit as it developed.[11]

Nevertheless, Joubert adds: "When I say 'matter is an appearance,' I do not mean to challenge its reality, but on the contrary to give a true idea of its real tenuousness" (*Carnets*, 1: 235). Thus the solid is just a transitory state. It tends toward its primary dissolution. Joubert's world is a vast cloud. For him things ineluctably return to a state of evanescence: "All of matter is pliable, or meltable or malleable, or everything can be divided into invisible, impalpable parts, by crushing or pulverization in the case of a solid body, or if already fluid, by evaporation. Marble or lead can become a cloud, from evaporation to evaporation" (*Carnets*, 1: 236–237). The elements are mixed together in a common aerial, ethereal origin: "In the movement from high to low, ether becomes fire, fire becomes air, air becomes water, water becomes earth. And in the movement from low to high, earth becomes water, water becomes air, air becomes fire, fire becomes ether" (*Carnets*, 1: 220). All of this takes place on a corpuscular, elemental level: "In a grain of sand, there is fire, water, air and dust" (*Carnets*, 1: 220). In the same spirit, Joubert favors the light and the weak. For him strength is always feeble: "The light dominates the heavy" (*Carnets*, 1: 220). The writer of laziness, the thinker of repose, remains perfectly consistent.

Joubert's aesthetics, in tune with this aerial physics, obeys the imperative of all that is light. Joubert's letter is ethereal, gossamer. Poetry, his ideal form of writing, takes shape in opposition to solid matter. It is the jubilation of the air. Clearly, Joubert could only be a writer of the discontinuous; his prose can only trace the inflexion of the minimal, the temptation of nothing: "The transparent, the diaphanous, the merest bit of matter, the magical; the imitation of the divine that created all things from little and, so to speak, from nothing: this is one of the essential characteristics of poetry" (*Carnets*, 1: 319). Poetry is the redemption of the air: "In our style (or in our written language) there must always be voice, soul, space, open air, words that subsist on their own, that carry their own place with them" (*Carnets*, 2: 535). Poetry offers the best ordering of appearance; it corresponds to this tenuousness of matter, it represents the excellence of little: "Poetry constructs with minimal matter: with leaves, with grains of sand, with air, with nothings, etc." (*Carnets*, 2: 735).

Vapor again appears as a metaphor in Joubert's characterization of conversation, which is a liquid expression, a spiritual volatilization of individuals. Joubert's motto becomes as follows: "To skim the froth of one's wit, every day. In Paris this transformation is accomplished through conversation and through a sort of bubbling produced without fail by the commerce of witty people" (*Carnets*, 2: 717). Conversational communication is an intermingling of sighs and flames. Thus, Joubert's orator must be able to show his wit; and intelligence is a purely gaseous, subtle effect:

"Our intelligence radiates and our sensibility is surrounded by a vapor. In short man has an atmosphere of his own" (*Carnets*, 2: 791). Likewise, seen in chemical terms, the voice is conceived not only in its acoustical dimension; in Joubert's definition it is a blend of the aerial and the gaseous: "But the voice is not merely air, but air shaped by us, imbued with our warmth and enveloped in a sort of skin by the vapor of our internal atmosphere" (*Carnets*, 1: 198). Joubert's aerial metamorphoses could be phrased in Deleuzian terms as a "becoming-butterfly": "Indeed, in many ways I am like a butterfly" (*Carnets*, 1: 371). Other winged creatures also exert their attraction: "Desire to be a bird, a bee. Man senses that his happiness is in the air" (*Carnets*, 1: 178). Joubert dreams of being Daedalus (*Carnets*, 1: 188).

When Joubert champions the French spirit over the German spirit, what counts for him is the difference between the light and the heavy. The model for this solidity, which also leads to obscurity, is Kant. Mentioning Kant's heaviness, the density of his discourse, Joubert concludes that it is "painful to hear" (*Carnets*, 2: 297). In this context, the distinction also amounts to one between brevity and volume:

> A French mind would say in one line, one word, what [Kant] can barely say in a whole volume; a creator of opaque shadows who, seduced and seducing others by this very opacity, believes and induces belief that there is in his obscure abstractions a solidity which in truth is not there. . . . I will rack my brain again, and yet again, against these pebbles, this iron, these eggs of stone, this granite.
> (*Lettres à Pauline de Beaumont*, p. 54)

Joubert's prescription for the German genius is the nonchalance of the French spirit. His attachment to the thinking of the ancient philosophers follows the same logic: "I prefer their clouds to our pebbles. If we had condensed and fixed the air, would it be any better to breathe? The spirit needs mists, subtleties, fluids" (*Car-*

nets, 2: 696). In this sense, a model for the French spirit as Joubert sees it would be the Marivaux introduced at the beginning of this study. As we have seen, he too elected the physics of the liquid over that of concretion. Marivaux's *bagatelle* or trifle has much in common with Joubert's lightness of touch: both breathe the spirit of evaporation, of the sublime. Like Joubert, Marivaux recoiled from the *magnum opus*. He ushered in that other, lighter, eighteenth century, running counter to the Enlightenment annealed in the forward march of progress, in system and rationalization. And in the tradition of the ancients, the distinction made by Josef Pieper between *ratio* and *intellectus* (*Leisure*, pp. 30–31) holds not only for Marivaux but for Joubert, who himself distinguishes between "to know" and "to reflect." For Joubert, reflection is labor, whereas knowing belongs to the intellectual regime of vision. He writes: "Nothing is so taxing to children as reflection. This is because the final and essential destination of the soul is to see, to know and not to reflect. To reflect is one of life's labors, a means of arriving, a pathway, a passage, and not a center" (*Carnets*, 1: 354).

If Joubert has never written a book, those he has dreamed have the virtue of brevity, the delicacy and genius of the minimal: "Short books are more durable than long ones. Booksellers revere large books; readers like small ones. The exquisite is worth more than the plentiful. A book that shows a spirit is worth more than one that shows only its subject" (*Carnets*, 2: 601). Books of the former type—veritable "diamonds" (*Carnets*, 1: 385)—are the ones Joubert liked to give as presents to Madame de Vintimille. It is as if a small book is the perfect receptacle for the spirit. The more voluminous a book becomes, the more it approaches condensation; it becomes bloated with its own matter. Hence the appeal of the short work, which assures the pleasure of reading: "Happy is the writer who can make a beautiful little book. Virgil and Horace wrote no more than one volume each; nor did Homer, nor Aeschylus, Sophocles, Euripides, or Terence. . . .

Menander, who is enchanting, is reduced to a few leaves" (*Carnets*, 2: 823).

With his frail constitution, susceptible to colds, Joubert was fond of his bed. He sought tranquility. In a letter to Pauline de Beaumont he extolled the virtues of rest, while criticizing people who bustle with activity:

> The world is at the mercy of happenstance. Those who claim to stop it, by throwing the gravel and fine sand of their little schemes into its waves, are ignorant of all things. To them I prefer by far someone who modestly entertains himself in his idle hours by making ripples in his well. At least he believes himself to be useless. The others believe in their own importance, and God knows how much time, thought, and talent they waste in trying to become so! I see nothing in them but a craving for bustle and movement ... Accord rest your love, esteem, and veneration. (*Lettres à Pauline de Beaumont*, p. 29)

It is in this light that we must read Joubert's criticism of Voltaire in the *Carnets*. Voltaire is the quintessentially restless philosopher, frenetic with ambition (*Carnets*, 1: 243): "A mind that never rested" (*Carnets*, 1: 233). But through Voltaire, it is the whole eighteenth century, the century of Enlightenment, that Joubert is criticizing—the century of industry par excellence. In the ideology of progress, which is the watchword of the century, Joubert sees a universe of machines, and he drives home the point ironically: "Hammers, anvils, rulers, compasses, containers and retorts are not even candles, let alone lamps" (*Carnets*, 2: 884).[12] In taking on Newton, Voltaire, and Kant, Joubert denounces the holy trinity that reigns over the Enlightenment. These three names join forces in upholding the mechanist ideology against which Joubert never ceased to write. Ruled by measurement and systematic rationality, they comprise the extreme opposite of the fragile poetry of the world.

In Praise of Rest

Mallarmé is often invoked in discussions of Joubert. I would like to compare Joubert to another, more recent, author: Roland Barthes. He too is drawn to the light, the weak, the tenuous. Like Joubert, Barthes is an apologist of rest. Barthes constructs a whole aesthetics of tranquility, withdrawal, and laziness, which he approaches through the lens of Taoism. In his course on *The Neutral*, where he develops his imaginary of withdrawal (he prefers the term "retirement"),[13] one of the illustrations Barthes uses is the Rousseau of the *Rêveries*. Barthes recalls the *far niente* of the fifth promenade with its goal of peaceful existence (*The Neutral*, pp. 138–140). For Barthes, Rousseau's idleness belongs to the horizon of the neutral as a pacific endeavor, a retreat from combative intellectualism.

Barthes's version of retirement can be understood within Joubert's framework of apathy. Barthes describes a series of postures of feebleness, of the meditating body submitting to a lack of either will or property. One posture in particular recalls Joubert: this is the "to be sitting" (*The Neutral*, p. 185) of the Tao—the very posture of laziness. It combines contemplation and wakefulness at the same time, entering into the same dream realm, the daydream. Barthes invokes a Zen formula, the dazzling maxim of apathy: "Sitting quietly, doing nothing" (p. 185). The equivalent can be found in one of the briefest "thoughts" in Joubert's *Carnets*: "To warm oneself in the sun of laziness" (*Carnets*, 1: 191), and even more clearly in his dictum: "The occupation of watching time flow" (*Carnets*, 1: 183).

The universe as recast by Barthes functions in slow motion. He is at once abdicating all responsibility, exiting the egotistical theater of ambition, renouncing the strategies of arrogance. His "doing nothing" is the symbolic injunction of the inactive, the cultivation of the minimum. Barthes once more joins Rousseau in this decision which he calls abstinence, whose contradictory formula is "to do the do-nothing" (*The Neutral*, p. 180), in a domestication of radical repose.

Barthes is heir to the legacy of the "French spirits" admired by Joubert. He is a writer of delicacy, which for him also lies in avoiding the burden of ambition. Barthes, like Joubert, favors the liquid, the light, the weak. He launches his reflections in *The Neutral* by recalling an episode from Tolstoy's *War and Peace* where a soldier faints during the battle of Austerlitz. Tolstoy's character falls, collapses. The noise of battle no longer reaches his ears. He experiences a sort of lapse in which the spectacle of war becomes invisible to him: instead of the raging battle, he sees only how "those clouds glide across the lofty infinite sky":[14] repose.

Barthes and Joubert enact the same process of emptying, of impoverishing the world so as to release its essential lightness. Joubert dreamed of a house for his thoughts to dwell in—a building that he would never manage to complete. Barthes's house is also dedicated to the "unfinished," the "Imperfect" (*The Neutral*, pp. 244–245, note 59).

Joubert's fragmented work shows the "casual intelligence that flies haphazardly like a bee, alighting on its way upon a thousand objects without remaining on any of them, caressing all the flowers, buzzing with pleasure" (*Carnets*, 1: 654). This writer of the subtle is even, one might say, the writer of the sublime, to be understood in the context of his personal physics and chemistry. Barthes would have appreciated Joubert's definition of delicacy (which Joubert no doubt applied to himself): "Delicate spirits are all spirits, born sublime, that have not been able to take flight because excessively weak organs, or flagging health, or overly weak habits have clipped their wings" (*Carnets*, 1: 158). The cloud-writer exhibits a type of thought, a cosmology that could be termed angelic, in the sense that Michel Serres applies this term to substances that change phase, morphing toward the state of subtlety—apparitions doomed to immediate disappearance.[15] Joubert is in effect a geographer attached to vaporous constellations. He conceives of space as a simple platform whose fullness is split by emptiness: "And the stars are actually islands, surrounded as they are by air or ether;

aerial or ethereal islands" (*Carnets*, 1: 407). Elsewhere, he elaborates: "Picture our geographic maps. As the filled-in areas are divided by the empty spaces left by the seas and lakes, so the finite, if I may speak thus, is divided by the infinite, and movement by rest" (*Carnets*, 1: 250). Joubert's topography is hashed by discontinuities and breaches. The writer who saw man's origin in a "drop of water" (*Pensées*, p. 112) ended up with the same meteorological notion of life. Here again water, wind: "Our life is woven wind" (*Carnets*, 2: 796). Joubert sees life through the prism of multiplicity. His vital concept embraces unforeseeability, indeterminacy, and intermittency. Life is this mosaic, a gathering of fluctuations.

Georges Poulet, who saw things from the perspective of time, points to Joubert's anxiety over time as a continuous chain, as expressed in this passage he quotes from the *Carnets*: "Ceaselessly working forces, activity without rest, mouvement without interruption, agitation without calm, passions without melancholy, pleasures without tranquility! That means living without ever sitting down, growing old standing up, banishing sleep from life, and dying without ever having slept."[16] Joubert replaces this restless time, Poulet writes, with the time "of patience and slowness . . . The time of labor but also the time of abeyance, labor in abeyance" (Poulet, p. 97). This is what Joubert calls "pure" time, and it becomes for him pure contemplation, absolute cessation, even from the activity of writing—a time filled with air: "I surrender to time itself, to pure time. . . . Even my pencil rests, and my little notebooks, which had never left me, remain in a drawer. I no longer need to keep them on my nightstand, or in my pocket."[17]

Epilogue

Toward Moderation

The heroes of this book hardly typify the legacy of the Enlightenment. They are not workaholics, addicted to frenetic speed, compulsively busy—those to whom Rousseau applied the term "restless" (*Reveries, CW* 8: 56). Next to those movers and shakers who championed the spirit of Voltaire, transforming his values into an ideology of productivity and efficiency, the lazy cut a rather pathetic figure. Their aesthetics of the minimum, their desire for less, their calculated refusal of ambition, are unseemly. Today, elections are won by competing in the omnipresent field of action and speed. Laziness is castigated in the name of a labor that is newly upgraded in the context of authority, order, and respect. "Work more to earn more": President Nicolas Sarkozy's famous command is the rallying cry of the French republic's bid for self-renewal. Early risers are the darlings of society. In all this, the State reflects the passions of ambition, wealth, and newly created fortunes. No rest for the new workers! The expansion of wealth reclaims its rights with a view to shameless self-display. Even the machine of the State is required to demonstrate its own performativity; it runs nonstop. . . .The government has a horror of vacation, even when it ought to be at rest. The exercise of government must be a never-ending pursuit.

Laziness and politics are indeed incompatible. The eighteenth century offers a stunning example of this in one of its salient figures, Georges-Jacques Danton. In his play *The Death of Danton*, Georg Büchner brings to life this notorious member of the Convention. The play revisits the caricature of Danton as a pleasure-seeking epicurean, in sharp contrast to the severe Robespierre. Once seen as the heir to Diderot, Danton is presented as the incarnation of vice. One of Büchner's protagonists, Lacroix, echoes Robespierre's judgment, emphasizing the Jacobin valorization of work: "What's more, Danton, we're 'full of vice,' as Robespierre puts it, in other words we enjoy life, and the people are 'virtuous,' in other words they don't enjoy life, because the grind of work has blunted their senses."[1] Danton's epicurean maxim is quite clear: "Everyone behaves according to his nature: we do what we do because it does us good" (*Danton's Death*, p. 24).

Among Danton's vices, laziness has often been mentioned; it was to become an integral part of his legend. Danton did not write, he spoke. He was a brilliant improviser; circumstance brought out the best in him. As his contemporary Gohier wrote: "Danton never wrote down a speech or had one printed." He mentions how the famous orator joined the ranks of those who, surprisingly, have left no "works" behind.[2] Danton's publisher was in effect his disciple and secretary, the loyal Camille Desmoulins, who worked at the *Vieux Cordelier* and wrote in his stead, trying to hang on to "the rapid breathless quill and ride the revolutionary torrent full tilt."[3] The historian Alphonse Aulard, Danton's apologist, admits that Danton "never wrote."[4] His speech was entrusted to the ephemeral, to the spur of the moment. His ranting found its force in the present. He was not concerned with seeing his speeches reproduced in the press. Worse yet, the printed traces of his words that do survive are incomplete and adulterated. Aulard converts the very accusations made by Danton's enemies into praise, admiring the disorder, turbulence, and chaotic abundance of Danton's oratorical practices.

In the end, Danton's laziness is what sets him against the tide of Jacobin Terror. The Danton that Büchner depicts chooses to lag behind the brutal violence of revolutionary action, exclaiming: "It's unbearable. I wanted an easy life. I'm getting one too: the revolution's pensioning me off" (*Danton's Death*, p. 29). It is this "retirement," Danton's renunciation and dereliction, that his old friends will hold against him. Saint-Just enumerates their criticisms in his *Rapport* to the Convention: Danton's idleness in Arcis-sur-Aube, his sudden retreat, desertion, bouts of sleeping, in short his insolent *otium*: "What shall I say of your cowardly and continual abandonment of the public cause in the midst of crises, when you always preferred retreat?" (*Actes*, p. 543). Mona Ozouf mentions this particularity of Danton's career, his absences, which she also calls his "eclipses." Contradicting the legend passed down by Victor Hugo and romantic historiography, and revived by Büchner, Ozouf scrutinizes the calendar of events to correct the record on Danton's role before or after—but always at some remove from—the important dates. She stresses that "Danton arranged, prepared for . . . days that he did not experience."[5] Referring to Auguste Comte's writings and to Danton's own theorization of dictatorship, Ozouf draws a distinction: "When Danton resorts to force, he never elevates it to the status of a maxim" ("Danton," p. 136). In sum, she resolutely paints the portrait of a "colossus" who is fragile and tender, a man whose robustness is curbed by weakness (here she echoes Saint-Just's judgment). Danton's thunder is stifled by indulgence: he is a Hercules stunted by moderation. Henceforth the mythical hero belongs only to the imagery of revolutionary terror, to its colossal reverie.[6]

Danton's mentality of breakdown is at odds with eighteenth-century mechanics. In Büchner's play, Robespierre takes his inspiration from the mechanical efficiency of "the Genevan watchmaker" (*Danton's Death*, p. 6). Opposed to Robespierre's mathematical rationality, to the dangerous ideality of his program, the historical Danton proclaimed: "It is impossible to carry out a Revolution geometrically."[7] The efficient machine par excellence is the engine of death, the guillotine that adds victim upon victim. Büchner's Philippeau declaims the bloody arithmetic, the mad exponential multiplication of the Revolution: "Yet another twenty victims have been slaughtered today" (*Danton's Death*, p. 6). Danton himself chooses another, simpler, vision of life. Resigned to the abbreviated work, he proposes a new philosophy of little, with an accompanying condensation of pleasures: "Life is becoming an epigram, and why not?—who ever had the breath and the spirit to endure an epic of fifty or sixty interminable cantos? It's time to drink the paltry essence from minuscule glasses, not great big tubs—that way you get a decent mouthful, otherwise you're lucky if you gather a few stray drops in the bottom of the barrel" (*Danton's Death*, p. 30).

Faced with the action of the revolutionary committees, Büchner's Danton advocates repose. He willingly chooses to break down: "I would rather be guillotined than guillotine others. I've had enough, what's the point of us humans fighting each other? We should sit down together and be thoroughly at peace" (*Danton's Death*, p. 29). This peace or rest is indeed the hallmark of Büchner's play, which would behead the terrorist police-state through a deliberate slowdown. Danton, the Indulgent, is progressively carried away by exhaustion, invaded by a lethargy that leaves him waiting for a programmed, "mechanical" death (*Danton's Death*, p. 58). The great actor of August 10, 1792—date of the insurrection and assault upon the Tuileries palace—looks forward to the end of bloodshed: "I see no reason why we have to go on killing people" (*Danton's Death*, p. 23). Lucile's chagrin in the face of Danton's death sentence is also phrased in terms of cessation: "The stream of life should stop aghast if even a single drop is spilt. The earth should show a gaping wound from such a blow" (*Danton's Death*, p. 72). The words Büchner places in his protagonist's mouth reprise the reference to the void that Danton made during his trial, when he proclaimed to the tribunal: "My home is soon to be the void" (*Actes*, p. 562). In a state of exhaustion, as he envisions his final rest in terms tinged with pessimistic materialism, he describes death thus: "death is putrefaction pure and simple, in life we putrefy with more sophistication, more subtlety, that's the only difference!" (*Danton's Death*, p. 59).

Thus ends this book of characters at odds with the frenetic eighteenth century and its fascination with automata. I have taken a detour to seek out machines gone on the blink, organizations that have broken down by design. We have seen various failures of the body—in the face of hierarchy, power, utilitarian synthesis, and finally, deadly force. Each time, laziness has seemed an intelligent suspension of work. Emerging as a *contre-temps*, a counter-time and counter-sense of the world, laziness spurns activity as the sole destiny of man and civilization.

Notes

Introduction

1. "Paresse," in *Mon bonnet de nuit, suivi de Du théâtre* (Paris: Mercure de France, 1999), p. 538. Published English translations of French texts are cited when available; parenthetical citations provide French and English references in that order. Where no published English source is given, translations of French quotations are by Jennifer Curtiss Gage.

2. See Maurice Dommanget, Introduction to Paul Lafargue, *Le Droit à la paresse* (Paris: La Découverte, 2009), p. 127.

3. Antoine de Courtin, *Traité de la paresse* (Paris: Helie Josset, 1679), p. 285.

4. On the evolution of the meaning of laziness, see Jean-Marie Goulemot's article, "Du vice au crime social," in the *Magazine littéraire* no. 433 (juillet–août 2004), pp. 53–55.

5. Chevalier de Jaucourt, "Oisiveté," *Encyclopédie*, v. 11, pp. 445–446.

6. "Paresse," *Encyclopédie*, v. 11, p. 939.

7. See his *Dictionnaire des synonymes* in *Œuvres philosophiques* (Paris: PUF, 1951), v. 3, p. 199.

8. Max Weber, *The Protestant Ethic and the Spirit of Capitalism*, trans. Talcott Parsons (New York: Scribner's, 1952), part 1, ch. 2.

9. Benjamin Franklin, *Poor Richard's Almanack* (1732–1757) in *The Portable Enlightenment Reader*, ed. I. Kramnick (New York: Penguin Books, 1995), p. 490.

10. Michel Foucault, *Discipline and Punish: The Birth of the Prison*, trans. Alan Sheridan (New York: Vintage, 1979), p. 30.

11. See "The Theater of Industry: Claude-Nicolas Ledoux and the Factory-Village of Chaux," in Anthony Vidler, *The Writing of the Walls: Architectural Theory in the Late Enlightenment* (Princeton, NJ: Princeton Architectural Press, 1987), pp. 35–49.

12. See "Fondation," *Encyclopédie*, v. 7, p. 73.

13. Rapport du 30 mai 1790, *Procès-verbaux et Rapports du Comité de mendicité de la Constituante* (Paris: Imprimerie Nationale, 1911), p. 705.

14. "Sixième Rapport du Comité de mendicité," in *Procès-verbaux,* p. 512. During the same period, the Marquis de Sade rails against the establishment of poorhouses which encourage begging. Sade's republic is an energetic machine of perpetual production, in the image of matter; it favors action and movement, and excludes parasitic individuals (paupers, beggars, loafers). In *La Philosophie dans le boudoir*, Dolmancé points to the Chinese model: "There, everyone works; there, everyone is happy." *Philosophy in the Bedroom*, trans. Richard Seaver and Austryn Wainhouse (New York: Grove Press, 1965), p. 216. The government of the republic is itself in perpetual motion: *Yet another effort, Frenchmen!* (p. 296). On the Jacobins' educational program during the Reign of Terror, inculcating young children with the virtues of work, see Wilda Anderson's analysis of a report addressed to the Committee on Public Instruction and reviewed by Robespierre, in her article "Régénérer la nation: les enfants terrorisés de la Révolution," *Modern Language Notes* 117 (2002), pp. 702–703.

15. Emmanuel Joseph Sieyès, *Qu'est ce que le Tiers-État?* (Paris: Champs-Flammarion, 1988), p. 34; *What Is the Third Estate?* trans. M. Blondel (New York: Frederick A. Praeger, 1963), p. 54. On Sieyès' conceptions of work, see William H. Sewell's book *A Rhetoric of Bourgeois Revolution: The Abbé Sieyès and "What Is the Third Estate?"* (Durham, NC: Duke University Press, 1994). He shows how the priest adapts Rousseau's notion of sovereignty to his economic and political conceptions, substituting "universal labor" for universal will (pp. 75–80).

16. Annie Jacob, *Le Travail, reflet des cultures: du sauvage indolent au travailleur productif* (Paris: PUF, 1997); see chapters 2 and 3.

17. Jean-Jacques Rousseau, "Discourse on Political Economy," in *On the Social Contract, with Geneva Manuscript and Political Economy*, trans. Judith R. Masters (New York: St. Martin's Press, 1978), p. 224.

18. Voltaire, letter to Nicolas-Claude Thériot, 8 décembre 1760, *Correspondance,* in *The Complete Works of Voltaire,* ed. Theodore Besterman (Banbury, Oxfordshire: The Voltaire Foundation, 1972), v. 106, p. 361.

19. Voltaire, *Candide, Zadig, and Selected Stories,* trans. Donald M. Frame (Bloomington: Indiana University Press, 1961), p. 101.

20. Voltaire, *Lettres philosophiques* (Paris: GF-Flammarion, 1964), p. 173.

21. Denis Diderot, *Essai sur les règnes de Claude et de Néron,* in *Œuvres complètes* (Paris: Hermann, 1986), v. 25, pp. 364–365. In his preface (p. 18), Jean Erhard explores connections between this text and Benjamin Franklin's precepts in *Poor Richard's Almanack.*

22. Immanuel Kant, *Anthropology from a Pragmatic Point of View,* trans. Mary J. Gregor (The Hague: Martinus Nijhoff, 1974), pp. 141–142.

23. Immanuel Kant, "What Is Enlightenment?" in *Foundations of the Metaphysics of Morals and What Is Enlightenment,* trans. Lewis White Beck (New York: Liberal Arts Press, 1959), p. 43.

24. *De la nécessité d'adopter l'esclavage en France,* ed. Arlette Farge and Myriam Cottias (Paris: Bayard, 2007), p. 99. In their commentary on this anonymous 1797 text, Cottias and Farge protest the policy of governmentality, that is, the rationale of government proposed by the text, which sought to conflate the poor, beggars, and slaves. The editors see this as a concerted strategy of domination by the State's powerful elite.

25. This legislation, decreed by Louis XIV to regulate the practice of slavery in the French colonies, is discussed by Louis Sala-Molins in his book *Le Code Noir ou le calvaire de Canaan* (Paris: PUF, 1987).

26. Léger-Félicité Sonthonax, "Proclamation au nom de la République" (Au Cap Français, 29 août 1793), p. 2. On the ambiguity of this freedom, see Yves Benot, *La Modernité de l'esclavage* (Paris: La Découverte, 2003), pp. 219–220.

27. See Robert Mauzi, *L'Idée du bonheur dans la littérature et la pensée françaises au XVIIIe siècle* (Paris: Albin Michel, 1994), pp. 376–378.

28. Nicolas-Germain Léonard, *Œuvres* (Paris, Didot, 1797), v. 1, pp. 192–193.

29. Xavier de Maistre, *Voyage Around My Room: Selected Works of Xavier de Maistre,* tr. Stephen Sartarelli (New York: New Directions, 1994), p. 5.

30. Michel Foucault, "What Is Enlightenment?" in *Ethics: Subjectivity and Truth,* trans. Robert Hurley and others (New York: The New Press, 1997), p. 309: "a way of thinking and feeling; a way, too, of acting and behaving."

31. Hannah Arendt, *The Human Condition* (Chicago: Chicago University Press, 1958), pp. 79–93.

32. On vagabondage and indiscipline, See *Discipline and Punish*, pp. 290–292, and on resistance, "Deux essais sur le sujet et le pouvoir," in Hubert Dreyfus and Paul Rabinow, *Michel Foucault: Un parcours philosophique* (Paris: Gallimard/Folio, 1984), pp. 297–321.

33. Michel Serres, *Éloge de la philosophie en langue française* (Paris: Fayard, 1995), p. 146.

34. Gilles Deleuze and Félix Guattari, *A Thousand Plateaus: Capitalism and Schizophrenia*, trans. Brian Massumi (Minneapolis: University of Minnesota Press, 1987), p. 372.

35. See *A Thousand Plateaus*, pp. 370–372.

36. See also *A Thousand Plateaus*, pp. 488–492.

Chapter 1. The Surprises of Laziness

1. Charles Baudelaire, *Œuvres complètes* (Paris: Gallimard, Pléiade, 1976), v. 2: 695.

2. Walter Benjamin, *The Arcades Project*, trans. Howard Eiland and Kevin McLaughlin (Cambridge, MA: Belknap Press of Harvard University Press, 1999), p. 802.

3. Jack Undank aptly describes the status of Marivaux's *Journaux* thus: "[they] are not yet canonical reading, even though they may be the finest essays in French since Montaigne." *A New History of French Literature* (Cambridge, MA: Harvard University Press, 1989), p. 422.

4. Marivaux, *Le Spectateur français*, in *Journaux et Œuvres diverses*, ed. Frédéric Deloffre and Michel Gilot (Paris: Garnier frères, 1969), p. 114.

5. Michel Gilot, *L'Esthétique de Marivaux* (Paris: SEDES, 1998), p. 137.

6. See Josef Pieper, *Leisure, the Basis of Culture*, trans. Alexander Dru (New York: Pantheon, 1952), pp. 33–35. Pieper reminds us that Kant, confirming his distance from medieval thought, considers philosophizing as a

form of work—a difficult, even a "Herculean labour" (p. 37). In this connection, Pieper points to the principle of the philosophical act as stated in
Kant's brief text, "On a Newly Arisen Superior Tone in Philosophy": "the
law is that reason acquires its possessions through work" (cited by Pieper,
p. 32). Indeed, Kant emphasizes in his essay that the practice of philosophy requires toil; in fact "the discursive understanding must expend a great
amount of labor to analyze its concepts and then arrange them according to principles, and it must climb many difficult steps in order to make
progress in knowledge." "On a Newly Arisen Superior Tone in Philosophy"
(1796), trans. Peter Fenves, in *Raising the Tone of Philosophy: Late Essays
by Immanuel Kant, Transformative Critique by Jacques Derrida* (Baltimore:
Johns Hopkins University Press, 1993), p. 51.

7. For a philosophical history of the *vita contemplativa*, see Hannah
Arendt's illuminating remarks in *The Human Condition*, pp. 12–17.

8. If he is paradoxically a misanthrope, it is, as Peter France explains it,
this privilege of leisure and contemplation that explains his contradictory
social status and philosophical eccentricity and gives him the necessary
distance from moral speculation. See *Politeness and Its Discontents* (Cambridge: Cambridge University Press, 1992), pp. 77–78.

9. Marivaux, *La Vie de Marianne* (Paris: GF-Flammarion, 1978), p. 251.

10. On the debate about the format of the periodical, see the book
by Alexis Lévrier, *Les Journaux de Marivaux et le monde des "spectateurs"*
(Paris: Presses de l'Université Paris-Sorbonne, 2007), pp. 63–72.

11. Gilot and Deloffre point out that "The 1722 edition contained the
phrase: *une feuille volatille [sic]*. This word *volatile*, according to contemporary dictionaries, is used only in chemistry" (*Journaux et Œuvres diverses*,
p. 588). As my analysis will show, contrary to the conclusion of the editors,
perhaps this was not a typographical error.

12. Cited in Marivaux, *Théâtre complet* (Paris: Seuil, 1964), p. 23.

13. Michel Gilot describes the situation in which Marivaux places his
subjects as "the burning and ambiguous relations that they have with others
at a given moment" (*L'Esthétique de Marivaux*, p. 137).

14. Baudelaire, *OC*, v. 2, p. 691.

15. See the article "Fluide" by D'Alembert in the *Encyclopédie*, v. 6.

16. Zygmunt Bauman, *Liquid Modernity* (Cambridge: Polity Press,
2000), p. 2.

17. On the opposition between solid and liquid, see Michel Serres, *Genesis* (Ann Arbor University of Michigan Press, 1995), trans. Geneviève James and James Nielson, pp. 107–112.

18. On the word *volatile*, see Michel Serres, *Angels: A Modern Myth*, trans. Francis Cowper (Paris: Flammarion, 1995), p. 44. In *Les Messages à distance* (Québec: Fides, 1994), Serres develops the notion further: "The term *volatile* applies . . . to a substance that undergoes a rapid phase change, into a subtle state" (p. 13). Addison, who from the start played on the opposition between volume and loose leaf, and who defended the aesthetics of the discontinuous, the fractured, of the fragmented journalistic work, thus opposed medicine to chemistry: "The ordinary writers of morality prescribe to their readers after the Galenick way; their medicines are made up in large quantities. An essay writer must practice in the chemical method, and give the virtue of a full draught in a few drops." In *The Spectator*, vol. 1, ed. Donald F. Bond (Oxford: Oxford University Press, 1965), p. 506.

19. "Sur la pensée sublime," in *Journaux et Œuvres diverses*, p. 56, p. 60.

20. *Le Cabinet du philosophe*, in *Journaux et Œuvres diverses*, p. 336.

21. The *Encyclopédie* of Diderot and d'Alembert defines pulverization as a process "that brings about the disaggregation of solid chemical bodies, by reducing them to a multitude of more or less subtle molecules which adhere so weakly that they yield to the slightest effort, almost like fluids, or which together constitute that type of imperfect fluid, which is known to all by the name of powder." Art. "Pulvérisation," v. 13.

22. Regarding the way in which the *feuille volante* is constructed as an allegory for Marivaux's journalistic work, Suzanne Rodin Pucci's excellent analysis shows how Marivaux's narrator applies a principle of varied sites, diversified signification, and sensory mobility. Pucci's analysis elegantly conjoins the *feuille volante*, the powder, and the volatile. See "The Spectator Surfaces: Tableau and Tabloid in Marivaux's *Spectateur français*," in *Exploring the Conversible World: Text and Sociability from the Classical Age to the Enlightenment*, ed. Elena Russo. *Yale French Studies* 92 (1997), pp. 149–170.

23. *Lettres sur les habitants de Paris*, in *Journaux et Œuvres diverses*, p. 10.

24. Michel Serres, *Le Passage du Nord-Ouest* (Paris: Minuit, 1980), p. 43.

25. "Notice" in *Journaux et Œuvres diverses*, p. 109, p. 110.

26. *L'Indigent philosophe*, in *Journaux et Œuvres diverses*, p. 311.

27. Frédéric Deloffre and Michel Gilot recall in their preface that *L'Indigent philosophe* was written in 1727, and that between 1720 and 1727 the authorities passed a series of ordinances and decrees against "criminal idleness" (p. 272). Gilot cites the legislation in effect that sought to "prohibit begging and, as far as possible, *far niente* and idleness, which are the root of all crimes"; *Les Journaux de Marivaux* (Paris: Champion, 1975), p. 496.

28 Arlette Farge, *Les Fatigues de la guerre, XVIIIe siècle, Watteau* (Paris: Gallimard, 1996), p. 95.

29. On the virtues of *otium* for the Cynics, see the book by Michel Onfray, *Cynismes: Portrait du philosophe en chien* (Paris: Grasset, 1990), pp. 147–153. See also the essay by R. Bracht Branham, "Defacing the Currency: Diogenes' Rhetoric and the *Invention* of Cynicism," in *The Cynics: The Cynic Movement in Antiquity and Its Legacy*, ed. R. Bracht Branham and Marie-Odile Goulet Gazé (Berkeley: University of California Press, 1996), pp. 81–104.

30. See Michel Serres, *Le Passage du Nord-Ouest*, pp. 21ff.

31. *Lettre sur la paresse* (pp. 443–444), *Journaux et Œuvres diverses,* p. 443.

32. On the attribution of this text to Marivaux, see the article by Jacqueline Hellegouarc'h, "Ces Messieurs du Bout-du-Banc: *L'Éloge de la paresse et du paresseux:* est-il de Marivaux?" in *Revue d'histoire littéraire de la France* 3 (2002): 455–459.

Chapter 2. Chardin's Slowness

1. Cited by Marcelin Pleynet, *Chardin, le sentiment et l'esprit du temps* (Paris: L'Épure, 1999), p. 49.

2. See Norman Bryson, *Looking at the Overlooked* (Cambridge, MA: Harvard University Press, 1990).

3. Cited by Pleynet, *Chardin*, p. 9.

4. Cited by Pleynet, *Chardin*, p. 11.

5. René Démoris, *Chardin, la chair et l'objet* (Paris: Adam Biro, 1991), p. 81.

6. *Encyclopédie*, art. "Bouteilles d'eau" (*Physiq.*), v. 2.

7. Diderot, *Œuvres esthétiques* (Paris: Garnier, 1968), p. 484.

8. René Démoris, "La nature morte chez Chardin," *Revue d'esthétique* 4 (1969), p. 383.

9. See Michael Fried, *Absorption and Theatricality* (Berkeley: University of California Press, 1980), pp. 46–53.

10. Cited by Pierre Rosenberg, *Chardin 1699–1779* (Paris: Editions de la Réunion des Musées Nationaux, 1979), p. 232.

11. Rosenberg, *Chardin*, p. 280.

12. Denis Diderot, *Salon de 1765* (Paris: Hermann, 1984), pp. 23, 25.

13. Démoris, *Chardin, la chair et l'objet*, p. 127.

14. La Font de Saint-Yenne, *Réflexions sur quelques causes de l'état présent de la peinture*, in *La Peinture en procès*, ed. René Démoris (Paris: Presses de la Sorbonne nouvelle, 2001), p. 134.

15. Diderot, *Œuvres esthétiques*, p. 493.

16. Cited by Hélène Prigent and Pierre Rosenberg in *Chardin, la nature silencieuse* (Paris: Gallimard, 1999), p. 31.

17. Cited by Norman Bryson, *Word and Image* (New York: Cambridge University Press, 1981), p. 113.

18. See Bryson, *Word and Image*, p. 112.

19. Michel Serres, *The Birth of Physics*, trans. Jack Hawke (Manchester: Clinamen Press, 2000), p. 30.

20. Marcel Proust, "Chardin ou le cœur des choses," *Le Figaro littéraire*, 27 mars 1954, reprinted in *Comme Elstir Chardin . . .* (Paris: Altamira, 1999), p. 17.

21. On Chardin's self-portraits, his pastel works, and his "bâtonnet de poussière" (stick of chalk), see René Démoris's striking remarks in *Chardin, la chair et l'objet*, pp. 173–179.

Chapter 3. The Great Project of an Idle Life

1. On this aspect, see Denis Faïck, *Le Travail: Anthropologie et Politique. Essai sur Rousseau* (Genève: Droz, 2009), pp. 233–237.

2. *Les Rêveries du promeneur solitaire*, in *Œuvres complètes* (Paris: Gallimard, 1959), v. 1, p. 1000; *The Reveries of the Solitary Walker*, trans. Charles Butterworth, in *The Collected Writings of Rousseau*, v. 8: *The Reveries of the Solitary Walker, Botanical Writings, and Letter to Franquières* (Hanover,

NH: University Press of New England, 2000), p. 7. Citations of Rousseau in French refer, except as noted, to the *Œuvres complètes* edition, ed. Bernard Gagnebin and Marcel Raymond (Paris: Gallimard, Bibliothèque de la Pléiade, 1959–1969), abbreviated as *OC*; unless otherwise indicated, published English translations are from the Dartmouth College edition of *The Collected Writings of Rousseau*, series ed. Roger D. Masters and Christopher Kelly (Hanover, NH: University Press of New England, 1990–2010), abbreviated as *CW*.

3. *Discourse on the Sciences and Arts (First Discourse)*, trans. Judith R. Bush, Roger D. Masters, and Christopher Kelly, in *CW*, v. 2: *Discourse on the Sciences and Arts (First Discourse) and Polemics* (Hanover, NH: University Press of New England, 1992), p. 13, 14.

4. *Emile*, trans. Barbara Foxley (London: Everyman, 1993), p. 189.

5. *Letter to d'Alembert*, ed. and trans. Allan Bloom, Charles Butterworth, and Christopher Kelly, in *CW*, v. 10: *"Letter to d'Alembert" and Writings for the Theater* (Hanover: University Press of New England, 2004), p. 262.

6. *Plan for a Constitution for Corsica*, trans. and ed. Christopher Kelly, in *CW*, v. 11: *The Plan for Perpetual Peace, On the Government of Poland, and Other Writings on History and Politics* (Hanover, NH: University Press of New England, 2005), p. 134.

7. *Confessions*, trans. Christopher Kelly, in *CW*, v. 5: *The "Confessions" and Correspondence, including the Letters to Malesherbes* (Hanover, NH: University Press of New England, 1995), p. 169.

8. *Julie, or the New Heloise,* trans. and annot. Philip Stewart and Jean Vaché, in *CW*, v. 6 (Hanover, NH: University Press of New England, 1997), p. 453.

9. *Essay on the Origin of Languages,* trans. and ed. John T. Scott, in *CW*, v. 7: *Essay on the Origin of Languages and Writings Related to Music* (Hanover, NH: University Press of New England, 1998), p. 309.

10. Aristotle, *The Politics*, ed. Stephen Everson (Cambridge: Cambridge University Press, 1988), 1256a 30ff., p. 10. See also Hannah Arendt, *The Human Condition*, p. 82n.

11. *Rousseau, Judge of Jean-Jacques: Dialogues*, trans. Judith R. Bush, Christopher Kelly, and Roger D. Masters, in *CW*, v. 1 (Hanover, NH: University Press of New England, 1990), p. 144.

12. "To M. de Malesherbes . . . January 12, 1762," trans. Christopher Kelly, in *CW*, v. 5: *The "Confessions" and Correspondence, including the Letters to Malesherbes* (Hanover, NH: University Press of New England, 1995), 5: 574.

13. For a psychological reading of this paradox, see Roland Mortier's article "Paresse et travail dans l'introspection de Rousseau," in *Rousseau & the Eighteenth Century: Essays in Memory of R. A. Leigh*, ed. Marian Hobson, J.T.A. Leigh, and Robert Wokler (Oxford: The Voltaire Foundation at the Taylor Institution, 1992), pp. 125–134.

14. On this return of idleness to its nature, see Yves Vargas, "Paresse et friponnerie," in *Cités: Philosophie, Politique, Histoire* 21 (2005): 115–130.

15. From Diderot's *Le Fils naturel*, cited in *Dialogues*, *CW* 1: 99.

16. Walter Benjamin, *The Arcades Project*, p. 805.

17. Jean-Louis Chrétien shows how Malebranche initiates a tradition associating thought and fatigue: "Breaking with Greek thought, Malebranche makes thought into work: 'To gain the life of the mind it is absolutely essential for man to work his mind.'" See *De la fatigue* (Paris: Minuit, 1996), p. 50. Rousseau is closer to the Greek philosophy that places leisure, *skole*, in the same category with thought.

18. On this sovereignty of poverty, see Jérôme Meizoz, *Le Gueux philosophe (Jean-Jacques Rousseau)* (Lausanne: Antipodes, 2003).

19. This involuntary *jouissance* is opposed to the objectless *jouissance* represented by the "dangereux supplément" ("dangerous supplement") in the *Confessions* (*OC* 1: 109; *CW* 5: 91). Sexual self-love is a perversion of nature and at its origin it seeks artificially to make up for nature; it does not take into account the constitutional slowness of the subject. Onanistic *jouissance* is impatient. Derrida sees it as bypassing "the duration of being." See *Of Grammatology*, trans. Gayatri Chakravorty Spivak (Baltimore: Johns Hopkins University Press, 1976), p. 151. In the context of dysfunctionalities of the subject, Rousseau mentions another form of laziness, which consists of giving in to imaginary satisfaction, leaving aside the real object and waiting for substitutive energetic compensation: Jean-Jacques is "lazy in acting because of too much ardor in desiring"; *Confessions*, *CW* 5: 35). This laziness recurs in the erotic sphere as the cause of numerous fiascos endured by Rousseau, or in any case of his refusals to complete the act.

20. On the connections between walking, mobility, and the paradox of citizenship in Rousseau, see Celeste Langan's innovative work, *Romantic*

Vagrancy: Wordsworth and the Simulation of Freedom (Cambridge: Cambridge University Press, 1995), pp. 31–58.

21. Nor is Rousseau aiming at the Stoical objective of labor with the inspection and scrutiny that govern such examination as a practice of self-knowledge. See Michel Foucault, *The Care of the Self,* trans. Robert Hurley, v. 3 of *The History of Sexuality* (New York: Vintage, 1988), pp. 59–64.

22. In the *Confessions,* even the meting out of time is experienced as a lark. In the idyllic episode in the company of Madame de Warens, Rousseau describes his daily schedule at Charmettes, how his "way of life ... was distributed" (*CW* 5: 198), declining his day from dawn to dusk. But the temporal segmentation is never disciplinary. Study (philosophy, geometry, Latin), and even labor itself, lead to pure recreation. Thus Rousseau can read, but "without studying" (*CW* 5: 201). On this euphoric effect of time management, see Jean Starobinski's fine article, "L'Ordre du jour" in *Le Temps de la réflexion* 4 (1983), pp. 101–125.

23. Michel Foucault, *Discipline and Punish: The Birth of the Prison,* p. 30.

24. "Fragments de botanique" in *Œuvres complètes,* v. 4 (Paris: Gallimard, "Pléiade," 1969), p. 1250.

25. Cf. *Emile, OC* 4: 1250; pp. 106–7.

26. "My Portrait," trans. and ed. Christopher Kelly, in *CW,* v. 12: *Autobiographical, Scientific, Religious, Moral, and Literary Writings* (Hanover, NH: University Press of New England, 2006), p. 43; translation modified.

27. *Encyclopédie,* "Herbier," v. 8.

28. See Émile Callot, "Système et méthode dans l'histoire de la botanique," *Revue d'histoire des sciences* 18.1 (1965), pp. 45–53.

29. Letter VIII, 11 April [1773], "Lettres sur la botanique," (1771–1773) in *Oeuvres complètes,* v. 4, p. 1191; "Letters to Mme Madeleine-Catherine Delessert: The So-Called "Elementary Letters on Botany," trans. Alexandra Cook, in *CW,* v. 8: *The Reveries of the Solitary Walker, Botanical Writings, and Letter to Franquières,* p. 160. In these letters written to Madeleine-Catherine Delessert and intended for the instruction of her daughter Madelon, the teacher emphasizes observation rather than the naming of plants or the memorization of nomenclature (Letter V). Botany must not become a "science of words" (p. 144); it must never escape the imperative of *seeing.* Rousseau eagerly compiled herbaria, another quasi-feminine activity (most

of his commissions were from women, such as Julie Boy de la Tour, sister of Madeleine Delessert, and the Duchess of Portland). On these herbals "addressed to ladies," see Rousseau's letter to Malesherbes, 18 April 1773, *Lettres sur la botanique*, ed. Bernard Gagnebin (Paris: Club des Libraires de France, 1962), p. 194.

30. Letter to Antoine Gouan, 6 October 1769, in *Lettres sur la botanique*, p. 152; *CW* 8: 211. In her article "The 'Septième promenade' of the *Rêveries*: A Peculiar Account of Rousseau's Botany?" Alexandra Cook re-examines Rousseau's ambivalence toward botanical pursuits, and asserts his investment in science, or at least in its pedagogy. In *The Nature of Rousseau's "Rêveries": Physical, Human, Aesthetic,* ed. John C. O'Neal (Oxford: Voltaire Foundation, 2008), p. 25.

31. Here Rousseau is perhaps unconsciously taking aim at what is held up as the machine par excellence in the series of trades described by the *Encyclopédie*: the marvel described by Diderot in the article "Bas." This is also the most advanced developed industrial model of the eighteenth century. See Jacques Proust, "L'article 'Bas' de Diderot," in *Langue et langages de Leibniz à l'Encyclopédie* (Paris: U.G.E., 1977), pp. 245–272. I would like to thank Christie McDonald for having directed me to this source.

32. Hannah Arendt, *The Human Condition*, pp. 145–147.

33. *Discourse on the Origins of Inequality (Second Discourse)* in *CW*, v. 3: *Discourse on the Origins of Inequality (Second Discourse), Polemics, and Political Economy*, trans. Judith R. Bush, Roger D. Masters, Christopher Kelly, and Terence Marshall (Hanover, NH: University Press of New England, 1992), pp. 25–26.

34. Cf. Gilles Deleuze, *Essays Critical and Clinical*, trans. Daniel W. Smith and Michael A. Greco (Minneapolis: University of Minnesota Press, 1997), p. 71.

35. Here we observe the exhaustion of the general will. Indeed, the "unanimous agreement" (*CW* 8: 3) with which the *Reveries* open, and which was to reduce Jean-Jacques to isolation, is resolved in a lack of will, contrary to the ideal of the general will, the convention whose effects on the State Rousseau described as follows: "Then all the mechanisms of the State are vigorous and simple, its maxims are clear and luminous." *On the Social Contract, or Principles of Political Right,* trans. Judith R. Bush, Roger D.

Masters, and Christopher Kelly, in *CW*, v. 4 (Hanover, NH: University Press of New England, 1994), 4: 198.

36. Giorgio Agamben, *The Open: Man and Animal*, trans. Kevin Attell (Stanford, CA: Stanford University Press, 2004), p. 66.

Chapter 4. Paradox of the Idler

1 *Rameau's Nephew, and D'Alembert's Dream*, trans. Leonard Tancock (Harmondsworth: Penguin, 1966), p. 33.

2. Louis-Charles Fougeret de Monbron, *La Capitale des Gaules ou La Nouvelle Babylone*, in *Le Cosmopolite ou Le Citoyen du monde. Suivi de la Capitale des Gaules ou La Nouvelle Babylone* [1759] (Bordeaux: Ducros, 1970), p. 163.

3. *Letter to d'Alembert*, *CW*, 10 : 323.

4. See Raymond Trousson, *Diderot* (Paris: Gallimard, 2007), p. 163.

5. *Le Neveu de Rameau* (Paris: GF-Flammarion, 1983), p. 128.

6. Etienne Bonnot de Condillac, *Oeuvres philosophiques*, ed. Georges Le Roy (Paris: Presses Universitaires de France, 1951), v.3, p. 199.

7. Rimbaud, *Œuvres poétiques* (Paris: Garnier-Flammarion, 1964), p. 118. For more on this subject, see Kristin Ross, "The Right to Laziness," which places Rimbaud in the broader context of an ideological protest against work, along with, notably, Paul Lafargue and his *Droit à la paresse* (1880). In Kristin Ross, *The Emergence of Social Space: Rimbaud and the Paris Commune* (Minneapolis: University of Minnesota Press, 1988), pp. 47–74.

8. *Éloge de la paresse, dédié à un moine* (Paris: 1778), pp. 26–27.

9. This is not economic alienation, the negativity of the worker's condition under capitalism, which Marx criticized and from which he envisioned man's escape. In Diderot's dialogue, Rameau's laziness allows him, from the very beginning, to escape the productivist logic of work and activity. On the concept of alienation, see Karl Marx, "From the Paris Notebooks" (1844) in *Early Political Writings*, ed. and trans. Joseph O'Malley (Cambridge: Cambridge University Press, 1994), pp. 71–96. See also *Le Droit à la paresse*, the radical pamphlet against worker alienation written by

Marx's son-in-law, Paul Lafargue, who in fact sought to revive the teachings of Diderot. See Lafargue's preface to *The Right to Be Lazy; and Other Studies*, trans. Charles H. Kerr (Chicago: Charles H. Kerr and Company, 1907), p. 17.

10. But the person is already wearing a disguise or mask. As Thomas Hobbes writes, "from the stage [the word *person*] hath been translated to any representer of speech and action . . . So that a person is the same that an actor is, both on the stage and in common conversation." Thomas Hobbes, *Leviathan or the Matter, Forme, & Power of a Common-wealth Ecclesiasticall and Civill* (London: Andrew Crooke, 1651; Hamilton, Ontario: McMaster University Archive of the History of Economic Thought, 1999), p. 99.

11. Michel Serres, *The Troubadour of Knowledge*, trans. Sheila Faria Glaser with William Paulson (Ann Arbor: University of Michigan Press, 1997), p. 145.

12. Marcel Detienne and Jean-Pierre Vernant, *Cunning Intelligence in Greek Culture and Society*, trans. Janet Lloyd (Atlantic Highlands, NJ: Humanities Press, 1978), p. 42.

13. There is in the Nephew's parasitism something akin to the wretched luxury described by Georges Bataille in *La Part maudite*—a sort of scornful defiance in reaction to the vulgar capitalist drive, a refusal of the selfish, self-interested accumulation of wealth: "A genuine luxury requires the complete contempt for riches, the somber indifference of the individual who refuses work and makes his life on the one hand an infinitely ruined splendor, and on the other, a silent insult to the laborious lie of the rich." *The Accursed Share: An Essay on General Economy*, v. 1: *Consumption*, trans. Robert Hurley (New York: Zone Books, 1988), pp. 76–77.

14. Michel de Certeau, *The Practice of Everyday Life*, trans. Steven Randall (Berkeley: University of California Press, 1984), p. 37.

15. On the nomad, see Deleuze and Guattari, *A Thousand Plateaus*, pp. 380–382.

16. See *A Thousand Plateaus*, pp. 3–25.

17. Cited in *Rameau le neveu. Textes et documents*, ed. André Magnan (Paris: CNRS Editions, 1993), p. 225.

18. *La Raméide*, in *Rameau le neveu*, p. 134, line 111.

19. Cited in *Rameau le neveu*, p. 179, lines 145–146.

20. These titles appear in the review article *Nouvelles Pièces de clavecin* in *L'Année littéraire*. See *Rameau le neveu*, pp. 79–84.

21. Jean-Yves Jouannais, *Artistes sans œuvres* (Paris: Hazan, 1997), p. 13.

22. See James Fowler's fine treatment of this topic in *Voicing Desire: Family and Sexuality in Diderot's Narrative* (Oxford: Voltaire Foundation, 2000), pp. 128–129.

23. From the police report on the occasion of Jean-François Rameau's arrest, cited in *Rameau le neveu*, p. 212.

24. Cazotte, cited in *Rameau le neveu*, p. 222.

25. Magnan, cited in *Rameau le neveu*, p. 213.

26. Cited by Trousson, *Diderot*, p. 213.

27. *Lettres à Sophie Volland* (Paris: Gallimard, "Folio," 1984), p. 281.

28. Diderot, *Correspondance* (Paris: Minuit, 1955–1970), v. 5, p. 218.

29. Cited by Roger Lewinter, Introduction to "Regrets sur ma vieille robe de chambre," in Denis Diderot, *Œuvres complètes* (Paris: Le Club français du livre, 1969–1973), v. 8, p. 4.

30. "Regrets sur ma vieille robe de chambre," *Œuvres complètes*, vol. 8, p. 4; "Regrets on Parting with My Old Dressing Gown, Or, A Warning to Those Who Have More Taste than Money," trans. Ralph H. Bowen, in Denis Diderot, *Rameau's Nephew and Other Works* (Indianapolis: Hackett, 2001), p. 309.

31. Louis-Sébastien Mercier, *Mon bonnet de nuit ; suivi de Du théâtre* (Paris: Mercure de France, 1999), pp. 882–886.

32. Diderot, *Œuvres esthétiques* (Paris: Garnier, 1966), p. 510.

33. Charles Baudelaire, *Œuvres complètes*, v. 1 (Paris: Gallimard, Pléiade, 1975), pp. 280.

Chapter 5. Philosophy on the Pillow

1. Louis-Sébastien Mercier, *Le Tableau de Paris* (Paris: La Découverte, 1998), p. 117.

2. Maurice Blanchot, *The Book to Come*, trans. Charlotte Mandell (Stanford, CA: Stanford University Press, 2003), p. 52.

3. Joseph Joubert, *Les Carnets de Joseph Joubert; Textes recueillis sur les manuscrits autographes par André Beaunier* (Paris: Gallimard, 1938), v. 1, p. 135.

4. Joseph Joubert, *Lettres à Mme Vintimille* (Paris: Devambez, 1921), Préface, p. XLIII.

5. Joseph Joubert, *Lettres à Pauline de Beaumont et Louise Angélique de Vintimille* (Paris: Calligrammes, 1984), p. 116.

6. Pierre Pachet, *Les Baromètres de l'âme* (Paris: Hachette, 2001), p. 81.

7. Letter to Louis-Mathieu Molé in Joseph Joubert, *Pensées, jugements, et notations*, ed. Rémy Tessonneau (Paris: José Corti, 1989), p. 36.

8. Michel Serres, *The Birth of Physics*, p. 86. But at the time when Joubert was writing, Jean-Baptiste Lamarck (1744–1829) set himself apart by his interest in atmospheric effects such as mists, clouds, and winds; he proposed a typology of clouds. For his writings collected in the *Annuaires météorologiques* (1800–1816) and the article "Météorologie" (1818) which he wrote for the *Dictionnaire d'histoire naturelle*, consult the site of the Centre national de la recherche scientifique at www.lamarck.net.

9. Michel Serres, *Genesis*, trans. Geneviève James and James Nielson (Ann Arbor: University of Michigan Press), p. 103.

10. Barbara Stafford identifies a whole pneumatological current, viewing the life of the spirit through a meteorological lens, at the close of the eighteenth century. Among those who embraced this novel trend Stafford points to Novalis, who conceives of spirit as an atmosphere. In fact, a whole vogue of ethereal sensationism emerges, in the tradition of stoicism. See Barbara Maria Stafford, *Body Criticism: Imaging the Unseen in Enlightenment Art and Medicine* (Cambridge, MA: MIT Press, 1991), pp. 417–426.

11. Joseph Joubert, *Essais* (Paris: Nizet, 1983), p. 251.

12. On the criticism of the Enlightenment as the century of mechanically manufactured books, and of their scholarly distribution, see Étienne Beaulieu's fine book *La Fatigue romanesque de Joseph Joubert* (Quebec City: Presses de l'Université Laval, 2007), pp. 53–54 and pp. 103–107.

13. Roland Barthes, *The Neutral: Lecture Course at the Collège de France (1977–1978)*, trans. Rosalind E. Krauss and Denis Hollier (New York: Columbia University Press, 2005), p. 137.

14. *The Neutral*, p. 5, quoted from Leo Tolstoy, *War and Peace*, trans. Louise Maude and Aylmer Maude (New York: Norton, 1966), pp. 301–302.

15. Michel Serres, *Angels: A Modern Myth*, p. 44.

16. *Carnets*, 1: 178, cited by Georges Poulet, *La Distance intérieure* (Paris: Plon, 1952), p. 86.

17. From a letter to Molé, *Pensées*, p. 37.

Epilogue

1. Georg Büchner, *Danton's Death*, in *Complete Plays, Lenz and Other Writings*, trans. John Reddick (London and New York: Penguin, 1993), p. 22.

2. *Actes du Tribunal révolutionnaire,* ed. Gérard Walter (Paris: Mercure de France, 1968 and 1986), pp. 535–536.

3. Camille Desmoulins, *Le Vieux Cordelier*, ed. A. Mathiez (Paris: Armand Colin, 1936), no. 1, p. 44.

4. Alphonse Aulard, *Les Orateurs de la Révolution* (Paris: Cornély et Cie., 1907), v. 2, p. 107.

5. Mona Ozouf, "Danton," in *Dictionnaire critique de la Révolution française. Acteurs* (Paris: Flammarion, 1992), p. 133.

6. See Antoine de Baecque, *Le Corps de l'histoire* (Paris: Calmann-Lévy, 1993), pp. 376–381. On the link between Hercules and labor in iconography of the French Republic, particularly in the painting of David, see Lynn Hunt, *Politics, Culture and Class in the French Revolution* (Berkeley: University of California Press, 1984), p. 115.

7. Speech of 24 January 1794, in *Discours de Danton,* ed. André Fribourg (Paris: Edouard Cornély, 1910), p. 653.

Bibliography

Primary Sources

Actes du Tribunal révolutionnaire. Ed. Gérard Walter. Paris: Mercure de France, 1968 and 1986.

Addison, Joseph, and Richard Steele. *The Spectator.* Vol. 1. Ed. Donald F. Bond. Oxford: Oxford University Press, 1965.

Anon. *De la nécessité d'adopter l'esclavage en France* [1797]. Ed. Myriam Cottias and Arlette Farge. Paris: Bayard, 2007.

Anon. *Éloge de la paresse, dédié à un moine.* Paris: n.p., 1778.

Aristotle. *The Politics.* Ed. Stephen Everson. Cambridge: Cambridge University Press, 1988.

Cazotte, Jacques, "La Nouvelle Raméide." In *Rameau le neveu. Textes et documents.* Ed. André Magnan. Paris: CNRS Editions, 1993, 172–189.

Condillac, Etienne Bonnot de. *Dictionnaire des synonymes.* In *Œuvres philosophiques.* Paris: PUF, 1951.

Courtin, Antoine de. *Traité de la paresse.* Paris: Helie Josset, 1679.

Danton, Georges-Jacques. *Discours de Danton.* Ed. André Fribourg. Paris: Edouard Cornély, 1910.

Desmoulins, Camille. *Le Vieux Cordelier.* Ed. A. Mathiez. Paris: Armand Colin, 1936.

Diderot, Denis. "Regrets on Parting with My Old Dressing Gown, Or, A Warning to Those Who Have More Taste than Money." Trans. Ralph H. Bowen. In *Rameau's Nephew and Other Works.* Indianapolis: Hackett, 2001.

———. *Essai sur les règnes de Claude et de Néron.* In *Œuvres complètes.* Vol. 25. Paris: Hermann, 1986.

———. *Lettres à Sophie Volland.* Paris: Gallimard, "Folio," 1984.

———. *Salon de 1765.* Paris: Hermann, 1984.

———. *Le Neveu de Rameau.* Paris: GF-Flammarion, 1983.

Diderot, Denis. "Regrets sur ma vieille robe de chambre." In *Œuvres complètes*. Vol. 8. Paris: Le Club français du livre, 1969–1973.

———. *Œuvres esthétiques*. Paris: Garnier, 1968.

———. *Rameau's Nephew, and D'Alembert's Dream*. Trans. Leonard Tancock. Harmondsworth: Penguin, 1966.

———. *Correspondance*. Paris: Minuit, 1955–1970.

Diderot, Denis, and D'Alembert. *Encyclopédie, ou Dictionnaire raisonné des sciences, des arts et des métiers* [Paris: Briasson, David, Le Breton, 1751–1772]. New York: Pergamon Press/Readex Microprint, 1969.

Fougeret de Monbron, Louis-Charles. *La Capitale des Gaules ou La Nouvelle Babylone*. In *Le Cosmopolite ou Le Citoyen du monde. Suivi de la Capitale des Gaules ou La Nouvelle Babylone* [1759]. Bordeaux: Ducros, 1970.

Franklin, Benjamin. *Poor Richard's Almanack* [1732–1757]. In *The Portable Enlightenment Reader*. Ed. I. Kramnick. New York: Penguin Books, 1995.

Hobbes, Thomas. *Leviathan or the Matter, Forme, & Power of a Commonwealth Ecclesiasticall and Civill*. London: Andrew Crooke, 1651; Hamilton, Ontario: McMaster University Archive of the History of Economic Thought, 1999.

Joubert, Joseph. *Pensées*. Ed. Rémy Tessonneau. Paris: José Corti, 1989.

———. *Lettres à Pauline de Beaumont et Louise Angélique de Vintimille*. Paris: Calligrammes, 1984.

———. *Essais*. Paris: Nizet, 1983.

———. *Les Carnets de Joseph Joubert; Textes recueillis sur les manuscrits autographes par André Beaunier*. 2 vols. Paris: Gallimard, 1938. [abbr. *Carnets*]

———. *Lettres à Mme Vintimille*. Paris: Devambez, 1921.

Kant, Immanuel. "On a Newly Arisen Superior Tone in Philosophy" [1796]. Trans. Peter Fenves. In *Raising the Tone of Philosophy: Late Essays by Immanuel Kant, Transformative Critique by Jacques Derrida*. Baltimore: Johns Hopkins University Press, 1993.

———. *Anthropology from a Pragmatic Point of View*. Trans. Mary J. Gregor. The Hague: Martinus Nijhoff, 1974.

———. "What Is Enlightenment?" In *Foundations of the Metaphysics of Morals and What Is Enlightenment*. Trans. Lewis White Beck. New York: Liberal Arts Press, 1959.

Lamarck, Jean-Baptiste. "Météorologie." In *Nouveau dictionnaire d'histoire naturelle*. Vol. 20. Paris: Déterville, 1818, pp. 451–477. Site Lamarck: www.lamarck.net.

Launay, M. de. *Le Paresseux*. Paris: Le Breton, 1733.

Léonard, Nicolas-Germain. *Œuvres*. 3 vols. Paris: Didot, 1797.

Maistre, Xavier de. *Voyage Around My Room: Selected Works of Xavier de Maistre*. Trans. Stephen Sartarelli. New York: New Directions, 1994.

Marivaux, Pierre Carlet de. *La Vie de Marianne*. Paris: GF-Flammarion, 1978.

———. *Journaux et Œuvres diverses*. Ed. Frédéric Deloffre and Michel Gilot. Paris: Garnier frères, 1969.

Mercier, Louis-Sébastien. *Mon bonnet de nuit, suivi de Du théâtre*. Paris: Mercure de France, 1999.

———. *Le Tableau de Paris*. Paris: La Découverte, 1998.

Procès verbaux et Rapports du Comité de mendicité de la Constituante. Paris: Imprimerie Nationale, 1911.

Rameau, Jean-François. "La Raméide." In *Rameau le neveu. Textes et documents*. Ed. André Magnan. Paris: CNRS Editions, 1993, 117–151.

Rousseau, Jean-Jacques. *The Collected Writings of Rousseau*. Ed. Roger D. Masters and Christopher Kelly. 12 vols. Hanover, NH: University Press of New England, 1990–2006. [abbr. *CW*]

———. *Emile*. Trans. Barbara Foxley. London: Everyman, 1993.

———. "Discourse on Political Economy." In *On the Social Contract, with Geneva Manuscript and Political Economy*, trans. Judith R. Masters New York: St. Martin's Press, 1978.

———. *Lettres sur la botanique*. Ed. Bernard Gagnebin. Paris: Club des Libraires de France, 1962.

———. *Œuvres complètes*. Paris: Gallimard, Bibliothèque de la Pléiade, 1959–1969. 4 vols. [abbr. *OC*]

Sade, Donatien-Alphonse-François de. *Philosophy in the Bedroom*. Trans. Richard Seaver and Austryn Wainhouse. New York: Grove Press, 1965.

Saint-Yenne, Etienne La Font de. *Réflexions sur quelques causes de l'état présent de la peinture*, in *La Peinture en procès*. Ed. René Démoris. Paris: Presses de la Sorbonne Nouvelle, 2001, 87–155.

Sieyès, Emmanuel-Joseph. *Qu'est ce que le Tiers-État?* Paris: Champs-Flammarion, 1988.

Sieyès, Emmanuel-Joseph. *What Is the Third Estate?* Trans. M. Blondel. New York: Frederick A. Praeger, 1963.

Sonthonax, Léger-Félicité. "Proclamation au nom de la République." Au Cap Français: De l'Imprimerie de P. Catineau au Carénage, près de la Commission intermédiaire. 29 août 1793.

Voltaire, François-Marie-Arouet. *Lettres philosophiques.* Paris: GF-Flammarion, 1964.

———. *Candide, Zadig, and Selected Stories.* Trans. Donald M. Frame. Bloomington: Indiana University Press, 1961.

Secondary Sources

Agamben, Giorgio. *The Open: Man and Animal.* Trans. Kevin Attell. Stanford, CA: Stanford University Press, 2004.

Anderson, Wilda. "Régénérer la nation: les enfants terrorisés de la Révolution." *Modern Language Notes* 117 (2002): 698–709.

Arendt, Hannah. *The Human Condition.* Chicago: Chicago University Press, 1958.

Aulard, Alphonse. *Les Orateurs de la Révolution.* Paris: Cornély et Cie., 1907.

Baecque, Antoine de. *Le Corps de l'histoire.* Paris: Calmann-Lévy, 1993.

Barthes, Roland. *The Neutral: Lecture Course at the Collège de France (1977–1978).* Trans. Rosalind E. Krauss and Denis Hollier. New York: Columbia University Press, 2005.

Bataille, Georges. *The Accursed Share: An Essay on General Economy,* v. 1: *Consumption.* Trans. Robert Hurley. New York: Zone Books, 1988.

Baudelaire, Charles. *Œuvres complètes.* 2 vols. Paris: Gallimard, Pléiade, 1975–1976.

Bauman, Zygmunt. *Liquid Modernity.* Cambridge: Polity Press, 2000.

Beaulieu, Etienne. *La Fatigue romanesque de Joseph Joubert.* Quebec City: Presses de l'Université Laval, 2007.

Benjamin, Walter. *The Arcades Project.* Trans. Howard Eiland and Kevin McLaughlin. Cambridge, MA: Belknap Press of Harvard University Press, 1999.

Benot, Yves. *La Modernité de l'esclavage.* Paris: La Découverte, 2003.

Blanchot, Maurice. *The Book to Come.* Trans. Charlotte Mandell. Stanford: Stanford University Press, 2003.

Branham, R. Bracht. "Defacing the Currency: Diogenes' Rhetoric and the *Invention* of Cynicism." In *The Cynics: The Cynic Movement in*

Antiquity and Its Legacy. Ed. R. Bracht Branham and Marie-Odile Goulet Gazé, 81–104. Berkeley: University of California Press, 1996.

Bryson, Norman. *Looking at the Overlooked.* Cambridge, MA: Harvard University Press, 1990.

———. *Word and Image.* New York: Cambridge University Press, 1981.

Büchner, Georg. *Danton's Death.* In *Complete Plays, Lenz and Other Writings.* Trans. John Reddick. London and New York: Penguin, 1993.

Callot, Émile. "Système et méthode dans l'histoire de la botanique." *Revue d'histoire des sciences* 18.1 (1965): 45–53.

Chrétien, Jean-Louis. *De la fatigue.* Paris: Minuit, 1996.

Cook, Alexandra. "The 'Septième promenade' of the *Rêveries*: A Peculiar Account of Rousseau's Botany?" In *The Nature of Rousseau's "Rêveries": Physical, Human, Aesthetic.* Ed. John C. O'Neal, 11–34. Oxford: Voltaire Foundation, 2008.

De Certeau, Michel. *The Practice of Everyday Life.* Trans. Steven Randall. Berkeley: University of California Press, 1984.

Deleuze, Gilles. *Essays Critical and Clinical.* Trans. Daniel W. Smith and Michael A. Greco. Minneapolis: University of Minnesota Press, 1997.

Deleuze, Gilles, and Félix Guattari. *A Thousand Plateaus: Capitalism and Schizophrenia.* Trans. Brian Massumi. Minneapolis: University of Minnesota Press, 1987.

Démoris, René. *Chardin, la chair et l'objet.* Paris: Adam Biro, 1991.

———. "La nature morte chez Chardin." *Revue d'esthétique* 4 (1969): 363–385.

Derrida, Jacques. *Of Grammatology.* Trans. Gayatri Chakravorty Spivak. Baltimore: Johns Hopkins University Press, 1976.

Detienne, Marcel, and Jean-Pierre Vernant. *Cunning Intelligence in Greek Culture and Society.* Trans. Janet Lloyd. Atlantic Highlands, NJ: Humanities Press, 1978.

Faïck, Denis. *Le Travail: Anthropologie et Politique. Essai sur Rousseau.* Genève: Droz, 2009.

Farge, Arlette. *Les Fatigues de la guerre, XVIIIe siècle, Watteau.* Paris: Gallimard, 1996.

Foucault, Michel. "What Is Enlightenment?" In *Ethics: Subjectivity and Truth.* Trans. Robert Hurley and others, 303–319. New York: The New Press, 1997.

———. *The Care of the Self.* Trans. Robert Hurley. Vol. 3 of *The History of Sexuality.* New York: Vintage, 1988.

Foucault, Michel. "Deux essais sur le sujet et le pouvoir." In *Michel Foucault: Un parcours philosophique*. Ed. Hubert Dreyfus and Paul Rabinow, 297–321. Paris: Gallimard/Folio, 1984.

———. *Discipline and Punish: The Birth of the Prison*. Trans. Alan Sheridan. New York: Vintage, 1979.

Fowler, James. *Voicing Desire: Family and Sexuality in Diderot's Narrative*. Oxford: Voltaire Foundation, 2000.

France, Peter. *Politeness and Its Discontents*. Cambridge: Cambridge University Press, 1992.

Fried, Michael. *Absorption and Theatricality*. Berkeley: University of California Press, 1980.

Gilot, Michel. *L'Esthétique de Marivaux*. Paris: SEDES, 1998.

———. *Les Journaux de Marivaux: Itinéraire moral et accomplissement esthétique*. Paris: Champion, 1975.

Goulemot, Jean-Marie. "Du vice au crime social." *Magazine littéraire* 433 (2004): 53–55.

Hellegouarc'h, Jacqueline. "Ces Messieurs du Bout-du-Banc: L'Éloge de la paresse et du paresseux est-il de Marivaux?" *Revue d'histoire littéraire de la France* 3 (2002): 455–459.

Hunt, Lynn. *Politics, Culture and Class in the French Revolution*. Berkeley: University of California Press, 1984.

Jacob, Annie. *Le Travail, reflet des cultures: du sauvage indolent au travailleur productif*. Paris: PUF, 1997.

Jouannais, Jean-Yves. *Artistes sans œuvres*. Paris: Hazan, 1997.

Lafargue, Paul. *Le Droit à la paresse*. Paris: La Découverte, 2009.

Langan, Celeste, *Romantic Vagrancy: Wordsworth and the Simulation of Freedom*. Cambridge: Cambridge University Press, 1995.

Lévrier, Alexis. *Les Journaux de Marivaux et le monde des "spectateurs."* Paris: Presses de l'Université Paris-Sorbonne, 2007.

Marx, Karl. "From the Paris Notebooks" (1844). In *Early Political Writings*. Ed. Joseph O'Malley, 71–96. Cambridge: Cambridge University Press, 1994.

Mauzi, Robert. *L'Idée du bonheur dans la littérature et la pensée françaises au XVIIIe siècle*. Paris: Albin Michel, 1994.

Meizoz, Jérôme. *Le gueux philosophe (Jean-Jacques Rousseau)*. Lausanne: Antipodes, 2003.

Mortier, Roland. "Paresse et travail dans l'introspection de Rousseau." In *Rousseau & the Eighteenth Century: Essays in Memory of R. A. Leigh*.

Ed. Marian Hobson, J.T.A. Leigh, and Robert Wokler, 125–134. Oxford: The Voltaire Foundation at the Taylor Institution, 1992.

Onfray, Michel. *Cynismes: Portrait du philosophe en chien*. Paris: Grasset, 1990.

Ozouf, Mona. "Danton." In *Dictionnaire critique de la Révolution française. Acteurs*, 129–145. Paris: Flammarion, 1992.

Pachet, Pierre. *Les Baromètres de l'âme*. Paris: Hachette, 2001.

Pieper, Josef. *Leisure, the Basis of Culture*. Trans. Alexander Dru. New York: Pantheon, 1952.

Pleynet, Marcelin. *Chardin, le sentiment et l'esprit du temps*. Paris: L'Épure, 1999.

Poulet, Georges. "Joubert." In *La Distance intérieure*, 80–121. Paris: Plon, 1952.

Prigent, Hélène, and Pierre Rosenberg. *Chardin, la nature silencieuse*. Paris: Gallimard, 1999.

Proust, Jacques. "L'article 'Bas' de Diderot." In *Langue et langages de Leibniz à l'Encyclopédie*, 245–272. Paris: U.G.E., 1977.

Proust, Marcel. "Chardin ou le cœur des choses." *Le Figaro littéraire*, 27 mars 1954. Reprinted in *Comme Elstir Chardin . . .* Paris: Altamira, 1999.

Pucci, Suzanne Rodin. "The Spectator Surfaces: Tableau and Tabloid in Marivaux's *Spectateur français*." In *Exploring the Conversible World: Text and Sociability from the Classical Age to the Enlightenment*. Ed. Elena Russo. *Yale French Studies* 92 (1997): 149–170.

Rimbaud, Arthur. *Œuvres poétiques*. Paris: Garnier-Flammarion, 1964.

Rosenberg, Pierre. *Chardin 1699–1779*. Paris: Editions de la Réunion des Musées Nationaux, 1979.

Ross, Kristin. *The Emergence of Social Space: Rimbaud and the Paris Commune*. Minneapolis: University of Minnesota Press, 1988.

Sala-Molins, Louis. *Le Code Noir ou le calvaire de Canaan*. Paris: PUF, 1987.

Serres, Michel. *The Birth of Physics*. Trans. Jack Hawkes. Manchester: Clinamen Press, 2000.

———. *The Troubadour of Knowledge*. Trans. Sheila Faria Glaser with William Paulson. Ann Arbor: University of Michigan Press, 1997.

———. *Angels: A Modern Myth*. Trans. Francis Cowper. Paris: Flammarion, 1995.

———. *Éloge de la philosophie en langue française*. Paris: Fayard, 1995.

———. *Genesis*. Trans. Geneviève James and James Nielson. Ann Arbor: University of Michigan Press, 1995.

Serres, Michel. *Les Messages à distance*. Quebec City: Fides, 1994.

——. *Le Passage du Nord-Ouest*. Paris: Minuit, 1980.

Sewell, William H. *A Rhetoric of Bourgeois Revolution: The Abbé Sieyès and "What Is the Third Estate?"* Durham, NC: Duke University Press, 1994.

Stafford, Barbara Maria. *Body Criticism: Imaging the Unseen in Enlightenment Art and Medicine*. Cambridge, MA: MIT Press, 1991.

Starobinski, Jean. "L'Ordre du jour." In *Le Temps de la réflexion* 4 (1983): 101–125.

Trousson, Raymond. *Diderot*. Paris: Gallimard, 2007.

Undank, Jack. "Portrait of the Philosopher as a Tramp." In *A New History of French Literature*. Ed. Denis Hollier, 421–429. Cambridge, MA: Harvard University Press, 1989.

Vargas, Yves. "Paresse et friponnerie." In *Cités: philosophie, politique, histoire* 21 (2005): 115–130.

Vidler, Anthony. *The Writing of the Walls: Architectural Theory in the Late Enlightenment*. Princeton, NJ: Princeton Architectural Press, 1987.

Weber, Max. *The Protestant Ethic and the Spirit of Capitalism*. Trans. Talcott Parsons. New York: Scribner's, 1952.

Index